THE
CHOICE

Other Books by Thomas E. Trask and Wayde I. Goodall

The Battle: Defeating the Enemies of Your Soul
The Blessing: Experiencing the Power of the Holy Spirit Today

THE CHOICE

EMBRACING GOD'S VISION IN THE NEW MILLENNIUM

by
Thomas E. Trask and
Wayde I. Goodall

ZondervanPublishingHouse
Grand Rapids, Michigan

A Division of HarperCollins*Publishers*

The Choice
Copyright © 1999 by Thomas E. Trask and Wayde I. Goodall
Also published in Spanish by Vida Publishers, ISBN 0-829-72169-X

Requests for information should be addressed to:
📖ZondervanPublishingHouse
Grand Rapids, Michigan 49530

Library of Congress Cataloging-in-Publication Data

Trask, Thomas. E
 The choice : embracing God's vision in the new millennium / Thomas E. Trask
 and Wayde I. Goodall.
  p. cm.
 Includes bibliographical references.
 ISBN 0-310-227844
 1. Evangelistic work. I. Goodall, Wayde I. II. Title.
 BV3790.T683 1999
 243—dc21   99-26080
                           CIP

Interior design by Sherri L. Hoffman

Printed in the United States of America

99 00 01 02 03 04 05 06 /❖ DC/ 10 9 8 7 6 5 4 3 2 1

Contents

Acknowledgments

W E ARE HEARTILY GRATEFUL to several talented people who have assisted us by coaching, preparing, and editing until the final manuscript was ready for print.

Rosalyn Goodall (Wayde's wife) is a college composition teacher who holds a masters degree in technical and professional writing. On each of our books she has tirelessly worked with us by utilizing her expertise as we have prepared the manuscript for the Zondervan editors. Her resourcefulness and labor of love have been greatly needed and are appreciated.

Jack Kuhatschek, senior acquisitions editor for Zondervan, has gently but firmly coached us along in each of our books with Zondervan. He is not only a tremendous editor, but has become a respected friend. Often Jack will suggest an article, book, or story that will add just what a chapter needs to give it a feeling of completeness. We sense that Jack truly loves his work and has convictions that continually prompt him to excellence and biblical accuracy.

Jim Ruark, senior editor, has worked tirelessly on our books as well. His expertise and dedication are greatly appreciated.

We are indebted to several other people at Zondervan for their constant encouragement: Dr. Stan Gundry, vice president and editor-in-chief; Joyce Ondersma, manager of author relations; and Sam Hooks, promotions manager. We also know there are numerous talented people who serve behind the scenes, and to all we are grateful. Just as the body of Christ needs every member to utilize his or her talents for God's kingdom, so, too, when a book finally gets to the bookstore, it is because there are many people who have sacrificially given to the process.

PERMISSIONS

The authors are grateful to the following publishers and persons for permission to quote from their publications:

Dan Van Veen, "Only Jesus," *American Horizon* (September/October 1998), published by the General Council of the Assemblies of God, Springfield, Missouri.

David Wilkerson, "The Forgotten, Lost Multitudes," *Time Square Church Pulpit Series*, 30 June 1997.

George Barna, *Evangelism That Works*, copyright © 1995, published by Regal Books, Ventura, California.

James Bilton, "God Doesn't Play Games," *The Pentecostal Evangel* (6 July 1997), published by the General Council of the Assemblies of God, Springfield, Missouri.

Ted W. Engstrom and Norman B. Rohrer, *Making the Right Choices*, copyright 1993, published by Thomas Nelson Publishers, Nashville, Tennessee.

Walt Mueller, "Marilyn Manson's Revenge," *New Man* (September/October 1998), published by Strang Communications Company, Lake Mary, Florida.

Introduction

W HY ISN'T THE CHURCH in the United States growing? In many places around the world, we see Christianity growing in unprecedented numbers; however, in America we are at a standstill. Church attendance has suffered a five-year decline, sinking to its lowest level in two decades. In a recent survey, only 37 percent of Americans reported going to church on a given Sunday. Attendance peaked in 1991 at 49 percent, dropping to 47 percent in 1992, 45 percent in 1993, 42 percent in 1995, and is now at 37 percent. W. Charles Arn, president of Church Growth, Inc., reports that not one county in the United States has a higher percentage of churched persons than it did ten years ago.[1] According to pollster George Barna, "We are seeing Christian churches lose entire segments of population: men, singles, empty nesters ... and people who were raised in mainline Protestant churches.[2]

In the periodical *Monday Morning Reality Check*, Justin Long reported that Christianity "is losing its share of the total population." Long did add, however, that some of the different religious traditions within Christianity do have a higher growth rate. Independent and nonwhite indigenous churches have an annual growth rate of 1.6 percent; evangelical churches, 1.12 percent; Pentecostal churches, 1.3 percent. Great Commission churches, which focus on evangelism and missions, enjoy a 1.06 percent growth rate. Unfortunately, this group only represents 25 percent of the total number of Christians in North America.

Even the highest growth rates within the Christian traditions do not come close to matching the growth rates various non-Christian religions and philosophies are experiencing. In the U.S., Buddhism is growing at an annual rate of 2.75 percent, while Hinduism is winning converts even faster, expanding at 3.38 percent. Non-religious people have a growth rate of 1.1 percent, and atheists have a stable 2 percent rate of growth.[3] The *Christian Science Monitor* reported that "in just the last 10 years, the number of English-language Buddhist teaching centers has grown from 429 to 1,166. There may be as many as three to five times that many informal Buddhist study groups. Sociologists also estimate that between half a million and one million Americans of Jewish or Christian background (excluding Asian immigrants) utilize Buddhist practices."[4] *Newsweek* reported that "the estimated Muslim population in the U.S. is 6 million and growing. . . . By 2110, the number of Muslims will surpass the number of Jews in the country, making it America's second-largest faith after Christianity."[5] Mary Rourk of the *Los Angeles Times* stated, "With almost no fanfare, the United States is experiencing its most dramatic religious transformation in this century. What had been a nation steeped in the Judeo-Christian tradition is fast becoming the most spiritually diverse country in the world. 'More religions are being practiced in the United States than any place else,' says Paul Griffiths, a professor of philosophy of religions at the University of Chicago.'"[6]

Why is the Christian church as a whole declining in America while other philosophies or religions seem to be more attractive?[7] Could it be that non-Christians watch the lives of Christians and are not convinced that Christians are any different than followers of any other religion or of the popular New Age movement, and thus Christianity cannot fulfill their emptiness and search for the living God? Christian statistician George Barna thinks this is a distinct possibility. He recently wrote:

American society is attributable to the fact that relatively few committed Christians model authentic, biblical Christianity for others to observe and experience. However, this lack of influence through example is not an intentional rejection of the opportunity to be a role model or representative of faith. Christians do not influence the lives of other people, and consequently have little impact on the national culture, primarily because *they have failed to integrate their spiritual beliefs and their behavior. In the end, Christianity is perceived by most Americans to be a benign religious form that is largely irrelevant to their struggles in life. This perspective is facilitated by the behavior of Christians* (italics added).[8]

This knowledge might not set well with you; it didn't with us. However, we must wake up to the possibility that when our life does not demonstrate the reality of Jesus, then our verbal witness will have little or no effect. When people observe that our behavior demonstrates little or no difference from the non-Christian's, they likely will ask why they should become a part of Christianity or choose Christianity over another fast-growing religion, such as Mormonism, Islam, or the New Age movement, when they see stronger commitments, great sincerity, and lifestyle differences within these other groups. Barna comes to this conclusion: "Christianity is not losing influence in America because it is overmatched by the challenges of the day; it is losing its impact because believers have been unsuccessful at merging faith and lifestyle outside the walls of the church. Non-believers expect us to have different religious beliefs and practices; those differences fail to impress them. Only when those beliefs and practices shape our every other walk of life do they sit up and take notice."[9]

In America we have tried to Christianize all people. I have heard numbers that say as many as 80 percent of the people in America claim to be "born again." This is wrong. People might feel they are Christians because they are good, their parents are Christians, or they were baptized when they were a baby or a young child. But they have never made an unswerving commitment to Christ, had a life change, and borne fruit that gives evidence that they are followers of Jesus Christ.

This book is not meant to put readers on a guilt trip, but to serve as a reminder that we not only choose whether we will give our lives to Christ, but also whether we will grow in him and live so as to draw people to him. There is no question that the greatest forms of evangelism are personal friendship and family witnessing.

More than a church sermon, evangelistic crusade, Sunday school class, youth camp, or retreat, people look for another human life that demonstrates reality, communicates truth, and shows that Christianity is more than a religion; it is a living relationship with the Creator God. Forty-four percent of people who become Christians do so because of a personal relationship with a friend or family member.[10]

Recently I attended a Rotary luncheon and heard a leading educational expert from that state say, "The world has grown more in knowledge and education since 1930 than since the beginning of time until 1930." That alarming statement opened my eyes once again to the fact that there has never been a day like today. We live in a world that has experienced technological advancement beyond imagination and greater educational opportunities than we could have hoped for. Yet despite all of the world's progress, we face greater needs and challenges than ever before. Suicide is the number two killer of our teenagers, second only to automobile accidents. Could it be that kids see a very confusing world and decide that they want little—or nothing—to do with it? There is growing pressure to make it legal for doctors to euthanize those with terminal illnesses or the elderly who have an illness that will eventually end their life. If we could speak to those who want out of life, we would hear a host of reasons for their despair, but the haunting issue is that people are without hope. They have no reason to live and most likely have not experienced the Giver of life.

Someone has said:

> These are the times of:
> Fast food but slower digestion
> Tall buildings but short tempers
> Large computers but small people
> Steep incomes but shallow values
> National peace but domestic violence
> Faster planes but slower progress
> Greater knowledge but less satisfaction
> Longer lines but higher prices

More leisure but less fun
Newer TV shows but more boredom
Conquering outer space but not inner space
Two incomes but more divorces
Fewer children but more problems
Adding years to life but not life to years
Making more copies but having less to say
Taking more vitamins but having more colds
Being charged more but owning less

These are the times of:
Quick fixes but no satisfaction
Disposable diapers
Throw-away morality
Overweight bodies
High prices
Low morals
Narrow minds
Full stomachs
But empty faces ...
These are the times.[11]

Let's ask ourselves how we can choose to live in such a way that people will take notice. As we look at our lives, what would make someone without Christ want to know Christ because of the way we live? This is a tough question for all of us, but there is no doubt that we must ask it. Luke tells us that "the disciples were called Christians first at Antioch" (Acts 11:26). This was a nickname that meant "These Christ folk." William Barclay informs us that "it was a contemptuous nickname; but the Christians took it and made it known to all the world. By their lives they made it a name not of contempt but of respect and admiration and even wonder."[12] Our lives must demonstrate more than head knowledge; Christianity must be lived out not only for our own salvation but to show those without Christ the dramatic difference he makes in a life. As we face a new millennium and try to communicate the gospel to a new generation, what are the critical factors we need to understand? Our message must never change even though our methods will. What do those without Christ need to see in our lives? This generation needs:

1. People who not only witness with their mouths but also demonstrate with their lives that they have a relationship with Jesus Christ.

When speaking in Maui, Hawaii, a couple of years ago, I heard of a leper colony in Kalaupapa, Molokai. Curious about how many people lived there and about the history of the colony, I began to ask a few questions of people who were native to the Hawaiian islands. Molokai contains the highest sea cliffs and is one of the world's most beautiful islands. Yet a compound of people with deformed, almost animal-like features peer out from behind their doors, looking for anybody who might be walking through the compound. Only a few of them are there today, and one of the reasons is Damien DeVauster, a man from Belgium who ministered to the lepers in the late nineteenth century.[13] He has been described by Lieutenant Governor Mazie Hirono as a "world-famous humanitarian and apostle" and by U.S. Senator Daniel Inouye as "a great crusader."[14] Curiosity about this person and about the respect he has held for nearly a hundred years caused me to look into his life in some depth.

Damien wanted to help find a cure for the lepers. When others would avoid them, he would embrace them. When it was difficult to find anyone to minister to them, he had a desire to do little else. He would hug and kiss them like members of his family. He loved them and taught them from the Bible every day.

One day as Damien was pouring boiling water into a cup, the water spilled onto his bare foot. Expecting tremendous pain, he was startled in that he had no sensation when the boiling water hit his foot. For a moment he became terrified. Wondering what it meant, he took some of the boiling water and poured it on his other foot. He felt no sensation there either.

That morning he walked into the chapel with a new understanding about the people he served. No one knew what he had discovered and no one knew why he began his Bible study the way he did. Every time previously he had begun with the words "my fellow *believers.*" This day he began his message with "my fellow *lepers.*" Damien had contracted leprosy himself.

When Christian apologist Ravi Zacharias visited the leper colony, he noticed a grave marker with Damien's name on it and asked a woman if he really was buried there or elsewhere.

She said, "Sir, he's not buried here. He's actually buried in his country, Belgian, because the Belgian government wouldn't let us keep his body here." She continued, "But the people here begged the Belgium government to send him back, and they wouldn't. Finally, someone asked, 'Will you at least send some part of his body so we can have a little bit of his memory in that physical frame that reached out to us?' In response to the request, the Belgian government severed an arm from the body of the corpse, and the arm is buried in Molokai under that marker next to the chapel."

Zacharias commented to his wife, "Isn't it fascinating that with a disease that desensitized them to any kind of physical touch they were still so sensitive to the reach of love?"[15]

The lepers of Molokai *saw and heard* a message from Damien that convinced them that his message was worth listening to—so much so that they wanted all that he could give to them.

When people look at our lives—the way we treat our family members, our employees or employer, colleagues, neighbors, and friends—do they see a life that looks like the Christianity we believe in? When others look at our values, marriage, or lifestyle or listen to our conversations, do they see and hear a life that demonstrates the love of God? What about our morals? Are unbelievers confused when they hear us say one thing and live another? A recent survey showed that only one out of three evangelicals believes that abortion should be illegal in all circumstances (although about six out of ten say that doctors who perform abortions should be imprisoned for murder). One out of four says that euthanasia should be legalized. Barely half (54 percent) say that gambling should be illegal in all locations in the United States. More than one-third (35 percent) say that the main purpose of life is enjoyment and fulfillment.[16] The old adage that actions speak louder than words holds true. Non-Christians who do not read the Bible see the walking Bible—the living Christian person. Christ in us is what they need to see.

Paul reminded the Corinthian believers, "You yourselves are our letter, written on our hearts, known and read by everybody" (2 Cor. 3:2). Barclay comments that "behind this passage lies the thought of a custom which was common in the ancient world, that of sending letters of commendation with a person."[17] He adds:

> There is a great truth here, which is at once an inspiration and an awful warning—every man is an open letter for Jesus Christ. Every Christian, whether he likes it or not, is an advertisement for Christianity. The honor of Christ is in the hands of his followers. We judge a shopkeeper by the kind of goods he sells; we judge a craftsman by the kind of articles he produces; we judge a Church by the kind of men it creates; and therefore men judge Christ by his followers. Dick Sheppard, after years of talking in the open air to people who were outside the Church, declared that he had discovered that "the greatest handicap the Church has is the unsatisfactory lives of professing Christians." When we go out into the world, we have the awe-inspiring responsibility of being open letters, advertisements, for Christ and his Church.[18]

GENERATION XERS AND PEOPLE in the new millennium will look to leadership that has a character that matches their message. Our day rightfully demands that the gospel message be seen as well as heard.

2. People who not only are able to debate their understanding of Jesus Christ and the Bible but surely know that their relationship is reality.

Many of us are skillful at debating our Christian beliefs. We know how to use the right words and verses to argue against gambling, divorce, homosexuality, abortion, and a host of other behaviors that are damaging to a person's life. We may, however, in our argument and debate, win the intellectual argument but lose the confidence of the person to whom we are talking. We may win the battle but lose the war. We certainly do need to know what we believe and how to support our beliefs with Scripture, but arguing will not win people to Christ. They must see that our viewpoint is something we deeply feel and that we share our beliefs because of the love we have for them. The sincerity in our voice will show that we are utterly convinced that what we are saying is more than words; it is our life.

I recently had the opportunity to visit North Korea. Our denomination is looking for ways to help the North Koreans with their food shortage as well as trying to begin ministry programs in that country. Daily I met dignitaries and Korean government leaders and heard their opinions about how they were right and the world (especially America and South Korea) seemed to be against them. My conviction that North Korea desperately needed freedom and an open door to the gospel grew as I witnessed their poverty and pain. When visiting the rice paddies one day, I asked a government leader if I could go into the water and plant some rice. I had not had this experience and simply wondered what was involved in the process. He requested that some rice plants be given to me, and I took off my shoes, rolled up my pant legs, and promptly walked into the muddy water to plant the rice. When I walked out of the water, I had numerous blood suckers on my legs and needed to remove them. I thanked the leader for the experience, and we moved on to visit the next place. What I didn't realize was that my activity impressed the leadership and the peasants. The fact that a "leader from America" would do this was something they did not expect. I was not aware that all North Korean people, from the top leaders to the lowest peasants, plant rice. They had the opinion that no American would ever do this. The activity helped them see sincerity and genuineness in me; I could not have planned it. This activity seemed to open a door for further discussions that we had dreamed and prayed about. Now, I could have argued my point about why Communism is bad and why they should permit Christianity to come to their country. A great deal of evidence exists to show that governments that choose Communism will fail, and that governments that permit Christian principles and truths to exist will be blessed. However, winning the argument would not have opened the door. They needed to know my feelings, my life, and my heart.[19]

When Ravi Zacharias was lecturing for the Evangelical Press Association in Chicago, he told a story about being in Budapest, Hungary, with a highly placed physicist. He said:

> We were in one of the halls where Madonna had done her taping for *Evita*. Half a dozen were sitting around the table with us; all of them atheists. At the table were two of my colleagues and my wife. The questions ranged from particle physics to the inexorable flow of evolutionary fury. This dialogue went on until nearly 11 o'clock that night. Finally, I said to the physicist sitting next to me. "Do you mind if I pray for you and for your country, because you've talked of the aimlessness of your young people?" He looked at the others and they all nodded. Here were atheists sitting around a table, and we bowed our heads and I led the prayer. I say this with God as my witness. When we opened our eyes, there were tears running down the faces of every one of those individuals. The next day they told us that most of them did not even go back to their rooms [that is, they stayed up and talked all night], and one of them made his commitment to Christ all alone in the lobby of the hotel. Later he said, "I was in the presence of something that I've longed for and do not understand. Can you help me?"

WHEN PEOPLE SEE HOW we really feel about the gospel rather than just witness us winning an argument, they will sit up and take notice, for they are looking for truth and reality lived out.

3. Christians who are not just concerned about the ends but the means as well.

Many people think that when Christians attempt to win others to Christ, those people are just a notch on the Christian's belt or a statistic. We desperately want to see each person come to a saving knowledge of Jesus Christ, but in our efforts we must not neglect the preciousness of each individual. All human beings are created in God's image and are loved by God. They are uniquely created and individually gifted, and they need to know that they have a divine destiny waiting to be released.

We must think of ways to reach a world that is technologically astute, accustomed to change, and ever seeking knowledge. The words we use to speak to this generation are critical. People have been conditioned to messages from a media that has discovered ways to speak to individuals through a television or movie screen. Media creators have found ways to personally relate to anyone who is watching and listening. Although we may not like what the music videos on MTV communicate, we have to agree that the fusion of music with video is the ultimate conquest of the imagination. Concepts are superimposed by pictures the producers want you to think about as performers sing. MTV communicates to a generation of people.

How is the church going to communicate the gospel of Jesus Christ in the new millennium? Never fear that the message will need to change—it must not! It cannot! The Great Commission is unchanged. God still says "come" to the unsaved and "go" to the saved. Our methods may change, however; the means we use to get to the end could look very different. One of the greatest communicators of our times, Billy Graham, has said, "Christians must also be open to creative change in trying new ways to communicate the gospel, whether by holding Saturday night as well as Sunday morning services or by developing new programs that meet specific needs."[20] Helmet Thielicke concurs: "The gospel must be preached afresh and told in new ways to every generation, since every generation has its own unique questions. The gospel must constantly be forwarded to a new address, because the recipient is repeatedly changing his place of residence."[21]

One new way of communicating the gospel to a new generation will most certainly include the Internet. H. B. London of Focus on the Family recently wrote:

Currently, four percent of teens use the Internet for religious or spiritual experiences. One out of six said that, within the next five years, they expect to use the Internet as a substitute for their current church-based religious experience.

Twelve percent of the adult population is already using the Internet for religious purposes, most commonly to interact with others via chat rooms or e-mail about religious ideas, beliefs or experiences. That represents about 25 million adults who rely upon the Internet for religious expression each month.

Our research indicates that, by 2010, we will probably have 10 percent to 20 percent of the population relying primarily or exclusively upon the Internet for its religious input. . . . Those people will never set foot on a church campus because their religious and spiritual needs will be met through other means—including the Internet.[22]

We live in one of the most exciting yet challenging times the church and the world have ever faced. We can choose to rise to the occasion and develop the means to reach the people of this age— who have the same spiritual needs as people in any age. Billy Graham sites four challenges we will face as we communicate the gospel in the new millennium.

1.   Excessive Urbanization: This means that poverty-stricken multitudes of the world's 6 billion people (50 percent who are under age twenty-five) will be living in large cities.
2.   Secularism will continue to supplant Christianity in former strongholds, especially in Europe, communicating a message that excludes God and moral and spiritual absolutes.
3.   Non-Christian religions are burgeoning where secularism isn't, with cults and non-Western religions proliferating in the United States and worldwide.
4.   Political changes can mean either open or increasingly aggressive closed doors to Christianity in the Middle East, Asia, Eastern Europe, and Russia, where the prayer

and partnership of Christian remnants are especially important.[23]

We must depend on the Holy Spirit to give us creative ways to communicate truth and stability to a very complicated age. All people are precious in God's sight, and in our witnessing to them they must hear the sure truth that God desperately wants them in his family. The means that we use to get to the end is critical.

What choices are you making today to show people that you truly belong to Jesus Christ? What moral choices are you making? What conversations are you choosing to have? What are you choosing to think about? These choices could be the greatest witnessing tools you have. If you feel convicted about your lifestyle, you can choose to change. It was Eleanor Roosevelt who said, "One's philosophy is not best expressed in words; it is expressed in the choices one makes. . . . In the long run, we shape our lives and we shape ourselves. The process never ends until we die. And the choices we make are ultimately our responsibility."[24]

Toward the end of Joshua's life he challenged the people of Israel about their choices. He said, "If serving the LORD seems undesirable to you, then choose for yourselves this day whom you will serve, whether the gods your forefathers served beyond the River, or the gods of the Amorites, in whose land you are living. But as for me and my household, we will serve the LORD" (Josh. 24:15). Joshua reminded his contemporaries that we choose the God/god we will serve. We choose our behavior, our lifestyle, how much we will pray, and how concerned we are about a world (our neighbors) that desperately needs Christ. Like Joshua, let us make the commitment that we and our households will serve the Lord.

Part One

TOUGH QUESTIONS

⋯⊙ ⊙ne ⊙⋯

What Do You Value Most?

I REMEMBER A DARK DAY IN RAVENSBRÜCK," said Holocaust survivor Corrie ten Boom.

> Betsie and I talked much with the Lord. Horrible things happened around us. There were days we said to each other, "More terrible than today it can never be." But the next day was still more terrible. Despair was on all faces, for there was no salt in any of the meals that day. When you are slowly starving, salt is very important.
>
> Several women died that day, one of them as a result of a cruel beating. The electric light had failed and after sunset we were in the deepest darkness. I put my arm around Betsie. She spoke about heaven and told me that shortly before we were arrested that she had read about heaven in a booklet. We had a talk with the Lord. He spoke and we listened; then He listened while we spoke. Then we went to sleep under the dirty coat we used as a blanket, and Betsie said, "What a wonderful day we have had. The Lord has shown us so much of Himself."[1]

Years after Corrie was released from the prison camp, she visited another type of prison in the tropical country of Rwanda, where it pours when it rains. Concerned about the prisoners during the rainy nights, she said to one prisoner,

> "Where do you sleep at night?"
> "Half of us sleep inside; the others must stay outside because there are too many prisoners." Some had a banana

leaf, others had a branch or an old newspaper to sit on. The uniforms were gray, and the faces were dark and angry. It was all so sad.

Could I bring here the gospel, the tidings of great joy? No I could not, but the Holy Spirit could. I prayed, "Lord, the fruit of the Spirit is joy. Give me an ocean of joy to share with these poor prisoners."

He did what I asked. I could almost shout for joy. I told them of a friend whose name is Jesus, who is good and so full of love, who never leaves you alone, who is strong and has the answer for all the great problems of sin and death. I said, "Perhaps you think, 'That is not for us, our lives are too terrible.' But I was in a prison where it was worse than here, where ninety-five thousand women were killed or died, including my own sister. There I experienced that Jesus is always with me. He lives in my heart; He has never left me alone."

I felt in my heart a great joy that imparted itself to the men who were sitting in the pouring rain. Then I saw that the joy of the Holy Spirit can be experienced in all circumstances. "This friend and Savior, Jesus, will live in your hearts," I continued. "Who will open the door of his heart to Him?" They all, including the guards, put up their hands, and their faces beamed.[2]

In the depth of her pain, Corrie ten Boom discovered an incredible truth: Joy and contentment can be found in the worst of circumstances. As someone has said, "Happiness is not the absence of conflict, but the ability to cope with it."[3]

What Makes You Happy?

WHAT DO YOU VALUE MOST? What are your goals? What do you think you need to do to achieve success? So many people—including Christians—think that true happiness comes from enjoyment in what we do, the fulfillment of what we own, or the security that we sense we have. If that is the basis of our happiness, then what happens when these things are taken from us? What happens when our security blankets are gone? Are we then able to say that we have a right to be miserable? Do we do anything we can to get that "whatever" that will make us happy? Masses of people—perhaps even ourselves—depend on something external to bring internal joy and happiness. Perhaps that is why so many are without hope and why many endeavor to numb the pain with alcohol, substance abuse, entertainment, sexual liaisons, or secret lifestyles.

In a book that became a national bestseller, *The Day America Told the Truth*, it was reported that "Most of us (55 percent) hide part of our lives from our closest friends. About the same percentage do things in the privacy of our homes that no one else knows about, that we would never tell anyone.... Americans hide, oh, how we hide ourselves—even from those closest to us."[4] And, we might add, people think they can hide from God.

The authors also reported:

> Everyone is making up their own personal moral codes— their own Ten Commandments.
> Here are ten extraordinary commandments for the 1990s. These are real commandments, the rules that many people live by.
>
> 1. I don't see the point in observing the Sabbath (77 percent).
> 2. I will steal from those who won't really miss it (74 percent).
> 3. I will lie when it suits me, so long as it doesn't cause any real damage (64 percent).
> 4. I will drink and drive if I feel I can handle it. I know my limit (56 percent).
> 5. I will cheat on my spouse—after all, given the chance, he or she will do the same (53 percent).
> 6. I will procrastinate at work and do absolutely nothing about one full day in every five. It's standard operating procedure (50 percent).
> 7. I will use recreational drugs (41 percent).
> 8. I will cheat on my taxes—to a point (30 percent).
> 9. I will put my lover at risk of disease. I sleep around a bit, but who doesn't? (31 percent).

10. Technically, I may have committed date rape (20 percent have been date raped).[5]

Today, many people have highly individualized moral menus. "We decide what's right and wrong. Most Americans have no respect for what the law says."[6]

Why are so many people breaking the rules? They may be saying to themselves, "Why keep the Commandments when no one is looking?" They get away with what they can and do what they want because they think that is what they need to do to be happy and feel fulfilled.

A deep sense of joy and contentment is available to every human being. It has little to do with what we own, where we live, our physical well-being, or our age. We believe that this "abundant life" is really what people are searching for. When the non-Christian world looks at Christians, they are trying to see if we really are all that we say we are.

Paul's Secret to Happiness

CONFINED IN A PRISON CELL and facing almost certain death, Paul wrote several letters to churches and people he loved. One such letter was to the Philippian church that Paul sensed would face incredible persecution, dark days, and an enemy who would endeavor to discourage and destroy them. Because of their faith in Christ, they were already going through hardship, and it would intensify. How would Paul advise them? What could he say to help them get through discouraging times? What could they look to when tough times came?

Perhaps it came as a sudden illumination or inspiration when he wrote the words, "Rejoice in the Lord always. I will say it again: Rejoice!" (Phil. 4:4). It is as if he is saying, "I've gone through just about all. What more can happen to me? Philippian believers, I know what I'm talking about because I've experienced it." He wanted them to know that the joy we have in the Lord is beyond all kinds of joy this world offers. Our Christian joy lies deep within.

The source of our joy is Christ, not our circumstances or the things of this earth. We can lose our material possessions, our security, our friends, and even our loved ones. We can be falsely accused, slandered, or worse; however, if our joy is in the Lord, we can never lose it, because Jesus will never leave or forsake us. C. S. Lewis said, "Joy is never in our power, and pleasure is. I doubt whether anyone who has tasted joy would ever, if both were in his power, exchange it for all the pleasure in the world."[7]

Paul had discovered the truth of how to be content in whatever situation he faced. He said, "I have learned to be content whatever the circumstances. I know what it is to be in need, and I know what it is to have plenty. I have learned the secret of being content in any and every situation, whether well fed or hungry, whether living in plenty or in want. I can do everything through him who gives me strength" (Phil. 4:11–13).

Henry Halley said this about Paul: "Joy is the predominant note of this Epistle. Written by a man in prison, who for thirty years had been mobbed, beaten, stoned, and cuffed about, enough to make the angels gasp. Yet he is overflowing with JOY. The very things which would naturally tend to make him sour only added to his happiness. It is simply amazing what Christ can do in one's life."[8]

As a believer in Jesus Christ, you can have this deep, abiding joy as well. Over decades of combined ministry to thousands of people, both Wayde and I have seen believers who have gone through incredible pain and suffering, yet they have an extraordinary kind of joy in their lives. In the last few months, I have visited Eastern Europe, Bosnia, North Korea, and Africa, where precious souls have gone through the kind of suffering that America has seldom (except perhaps in the days of slavery) seen. Yet in all of these countries there are Christians who have a unique presence about them, an inward joy. We are not necessarily talking about outward laughter (although it can include that) or a demonstration of happiness, but a deep, abiding sense of the presence of God in one's life.

Oswald Chambers said, "Man cannot find true essential joy anywhere but in his relationship to God."⁹ When a person has this kind of awareness, he or she also has a profound desire to share hope with others. In a sea of empty and meaningless lives, others will notice our joy and will want what we have.

Paul's exhortation, "Rejoice in the Lord always. I will say it again: Rejoice!" (Phil. 4:4), speaks of a *decision* we make, *discrimination* in whom we rejoice, the *duration* of our rejoicing, and the *demeanor* of our lives.

The Decision

"Rejoice"

Poetess Annie Johnson Flint lived most of her life in pain. She was orphaned early in life, later contracted cancer and rheumatoid arthritis, and suffered from incontinence. Those who knew her said that she was incapacitated for so long that she needed seven or eight pillows around her body just to cushion the raw sores she suffered from being bedridden. In spite of her pain, Annie found a way to have a phenomenal attitude. Her autobiography is appropriately called *The Making of the Beautiful*. She wrote a poem that was later set to music in which she reveals a deep sense of appreciation for God:

> He giveth more grace when the burdens grow greater,
> He sendeth more strength when the labors increase;
> To added affliction, He addeth His mercy,
> To multiplied trials His multiplied peace.
> When we have exhausted our store of endurance,
> When our strength has failed e're the day is half done,
> When we reach the end of our hoarded resources
> Our Father's full giving has only begun.
> His love has no limit, His grace has no measure,
> His power has no boundary known unto men;
> For out of His infinite riches in Jesus

He giveth, and giveth, and giveth again![10]

Like Annie, we can choose to rejoice even when life seems overwhelming. In fact, we can realize the benefits that can come from trials and suffering. British writer and social critic Malcolm Muggeridge said:

> Contrary to what might be expected, I look back on experiences that at the time seemed especially dislocating and painful, with particular satisfaction. Indeed, I can say with complete truthfulness that everything I have learned in my seventy-five years in this world, everything that has truly enhanced and enlightened my existence, has been through affliction and not through happiness, whether pursued or attained. In other words, if it ever were to be possible to eliminate affliction from our earthly existence by means of some drug or other medical mumbo jumbo ... the result would not be to make life delectable, but to make it too banal or trivial to be endurable. This of course is what the cross signifies, and it is the cross more than anything else, that has called me inexorably to Christ.[11]

Though life might seem overwhelming to us, we can choose to rejoice. In Paul's letter to the Roman believers, he wrote, "If God is for us, who can be against us? He who did not spare his own Son, but gave him up for us all—how will he not also, along with him, graciously give us all things? . . . For I am convinced that neither death nor life, neither angels nor demons, neither the present nor the future, nor any powers, neither height nor depth, nor anything else in all creation, will be able to separate us from the love of God that is in Christ Jesus our Lord" (Rom. 8:31–32, 38).

As believers in Jesus Christ we have something going for us that no other religion, philosophy, teaching, or psychological theory can offer. We have God on our side, and nothing, nothing, *nothing*, can divorce us from the love of God. His beams of love are constantly flowing in our direction. If, however, we believe that God's love excludes us from trials in life, we are mistaken. Difficulties and hardships can be our dear friends. Erwin W. Lutzer said, "We must accept the fact that God cares deeply about those in his family. Then why doesn't he prove his love? He does, but his values differ from ours. We value health; he values patience. We value comfort; he values peace. We value life without struggle; he. values faith in the midst of struggle. Thus, though he loves us, he doesn't exempt us from the tragic heartaches of life."[12]

No matter what we are going through or what might happen, we can "rejoice" in the fact that God is on our side. Whether we have much or little, whether we are well or ill, whether we make our goals or not—we can always be grateful and have the joy of the Lord. Compared to eternity, our earthly suffering is only a breath, so in all our circumstances, let's determine to be persons of praise.

The Discrimination

"In the Lord"

Our ability to rejoice comes because we can focus on the Lord rather than on our circumstances, career, or possessions, all of which are temporary. In Christ we have a sacred place where we can mentally and spiritually reside. If we value our careers, possessions, or comfortable conditions more than our heavenly treasure, we will only be joyful when we are successful, affluent, and comfortable.

Paul encouraged the Roman believers by saying, "May the God of hope fill you with all joy and peace as you trust in him, so that you may overflow with hope by the power of the Holy Spirit" (Rom. 15:13). Our faith and trust in the Lord bring an inner peace and joy independent from the trials we are going through, the events we are experiencing, or the positive or negative happenings we are encountering. At a time when the apostles could have been discouraged because they had just been flogged and ordered not to speak in the name of Jesus, they left "rejoicing because they had been counted worthy of suffering disgrace for the Name" (Acts 5:41).

Our salvation, hope, strength, and joy are in the Lord. After reflecting on God's wonderful creation, the writer of Psalm 104 expressed:

> I will sing to the Lord all my life;
> I will sing praise to my God as long as I live.
> May my meditation be pleasing to him,
> as I rejoice in the LORD (vv. 33–34).

When we think about how complicated life can be and the potential to become confused about what we should do, we can place our trust in the Lord, who is ultimate wisdom. James Dobson said, "Trust involves letting go and knowing God will catch you."[13] Another psalm says:

> The fear of the LORD is the beginning of wisdom;
> all who follow his precepts have good understanding.
> To him belongs eternal praise (Ps. 111:10).

As God's children, we can be assured that he has great pleasure in us. Constantly his eye of affection is on us. His ear continually listens for our prayers, words asking for forgiveness, help, intercession, and answers about life. Our thanksgiving and praise are like incense that he smells, and our arms that reach out to him are like children stretching their arms to a caring mother. God delights in us.

> His pleasure is not in the strength of the horse,
> nor his delight in the legs of a man;
> the Lord delights in those who fear him,
> who put their hope in his unfailing love (Ps. 147:10–11).

The Lord delights in people who are truthful (Prov. 12:22) and are blameless in what they do (Prov. 11:20). The prayers of those who live a righteous life are pleasing to him (Prov. 15:8). Zephaniah reminds us of the Lord's tender care for his children.

> The LORD your God is with you,
> he is mighty to save.

He will take great delight in you,
  he will quiet you with his love,
  he will rejoice over you with singing (Zeph. 3:17).

The Hebrew word for "rejoice over you" describes playful abandon or exuberant joy. I (Thomas) have never quite understood why or how our perfect, holy, merciful, and just God could feel this way about me. In spite of my failures and sins, he is always there, rejoicing over me because I trust him as Lord and endeavor to serve him in everything I do. If you are his child, he looks at you the same way.

The Duration

"Always"

When you feel that you cannot rejoice in anything or any other, you can choose to rejoice in God. Paul said, "I have learned the secret of being content in any and every situation" (Phil. 4:12). He knew that in spite of his circumstances, the Lord would always be with him. When Paul met opposition in Corinth, and people became abusive to him because he preached that Jesus was the Christ, he could have given up on that city. But the Bible tells us that "One night the Lord spoke to Paul in a vision: 'Do not be afraid; keep on speaking, do not be silent. For I am with you, and no one is going to attack and harm you, because I have many people in this city.' So Paul stayed for a year and a half, teaching them the word of God" (Acts 18:9–11). On another occasion when Paul was on the verge of being "torn to pieces" by a crowd because he spoke about the resurrection of the dead, he was protected from possible death by being taken by force to a barracks. He could have been disillusioned, discouraged, and ready to give up; however, "the following night the Lord stood near Paul and said, 'Take courage!'" (Acts 23:11). Later, when the ship Paul was aboard was in a fierce storm and about to sink, the Lord sent an angel to say to him, "Do not be afraid, Paul.... God has graciously given you the lives of all who sail with you" (Acts 27:23).

Paul knew that no matter what came his way, whatever happened to him, whether good or bad, whether verbal abuse or physical violence against him, God was aware of his circumstances and would be there to assist him. He understood that when the storms of life came—and they always do—the Lord of his life could calm the storm within him. The negative events of life didn't really make any difference to Paul because the Creator was with him no matter what.

Beside the verse "Do not be anxious about anything, but in everything, by prayer and petition, with thanksgiving, present your requests to God" (Phil. 4:6), D. L. Moody wrote in the margin of his Bible:

> "Our great matters are little to His power: our little matters are great to His love.
> Be careful for nothing.
> Be prayerful for everything.
> Be thankful for anything.
> Let your riches consist, not in the largeness of your possessions, but in the fewness of your wants."[14]

MOODY UNDERSTOOD THE PRINCIPLE of maintaining a sense of joy no matter what the circumstances.

When you have great friends, material possessions, health, and emotional energy, and everything seems to be working in your life, bathe all of these blessings with gratitude and a spirit of rejoicing, remembering that "every good and perfect gift is from above" (James 1:17). If you have not been in the habit of rejoicing, begin today. If you have been a person that has habitually rejoiced in the Lord, then determine that this will be a practice that you will always continue.

When you are around your family, friends, employees, or employer, demonstrate an attitude of gratitude and rejoicing. Emotions are contagious, and soon those who are often with you will display this same attitude.

When you are alone in your car, your home, in the night, or in your daily activities be a person who is thankful and inwardly and outwardly rejoices in the Lord.

The Demeanor

"I Will Say It Again: Rejoice!"

For many years I (Thomas) lived near Detroit, where I pastored Brightmore Tabernacle. If you fly over Lake St. Clair into the airport, the skyline is beautiful. While driving into the city one can marvel at the fine buildings architects have designed and gifted contractors have built. The idea for each building was at one time a dream in a person's mind. The architect meditated on the dream and planned how such a building could be built. The plan was then drawn out in intricate detail and finally skillfully constructed.

Detroit also has its rough, seamy, and ugly parts. In certain sections of the city, you could see a crack house or a motel where prostitutes make their living. You may even witness a drive-by shooting. The same kind of brain that in one person can imagine a beautiful building can in another person imagine how to do evil. This realization about the potential of people has always amazed me. The wonderful architect has a presence, a demeanor about him or her. So does the person who deals crack cocaine.

What makes one person go one way and another person go the opposite direction in behavior? Choices do not occur in a spiritual vacuum; they begin in a person's thinking and imagination. For example, a man does not decide in a moment to become a rapist or a murderer. He thinks about such behavior for long periods of time and finally acts it out (James 1:14–15). The same is true on the positive side. Architects imagine and plan buildings in their minds for years. The fantasies of our mind today are likely to be the actions of our body tomorrow.

What has this to do with us? As Christians "we have the mind of Christ" (1 Cor. 2:16). We can choose to think on all that God has done for us. We can imagine the wonders of his glory. We can dream God's dream, and we can walk (live) in the Spirit of God. Paul said, "Whatever is true, whatever is noble, whatever is right, whatever is pure, whatever is lovely, whatever is admirable—if anything is excellent or praiseworthy—think about such things" (Phil. 4:8). When

we do this we will have a godly demeanor or presence. We will be
known as a person who has a rejoicing attitude.

Paul was known for his joyful presence, especially by the
believers at Philippi. When he walked into a room, people could
perceive that his mind was focused on the Lord. As we look
through Paul's letter to the Philippian church, we can sense his
genuine delight in them.

1:4   He prayed for them "with joy."

1:18 He rejoiced that "Christ is preached."

1:25 He wished to bring joy to them by being with them.

2:2   His joy was complete when they were "one" in spirit and
      purpose.

3:1   He said good-bye with this encouragement: "Rejoice in
      the Lord!"

4:1   He called his converts his "joy and crown."

4:4   He reminded them to always "Rejoice in the Lord."

4:10 He rejoiced that they are concerned about him.

Joy is contagious. When those without Christ sense that we
have genuine joy, many will want what we have. When I began
college, I was not serving the Lord, and I had little joy. I might
have smiled on the outside, but I was miserable on the inside.
Only when I surrendered to the Lordship of Jesus Christ did I
find a sense of real joy. When Wayde was a young man, he tried
many of the things the world had to offer; however, nothing
brought him a sense of satisfaction or peace. He was looking for
answers in all the wrong places. One day someone told him about
Jesus Christ, and he responded by committing his life to the Lord.
Only then did he fill that void in his life. R. A. Torrey said, "There
is more joy in Jesus in twenty-four hours than there is in the world
in 365 days. I have tried them both."[15] Paul the apostle had experienced what it was like to have religion without a relationship with
Christ. Once he met Jesus, he was never the same.

Our sense of joy should be perpetual. Someone said that "the
calendar of the sinner has only a few days in the year marked as

festival days but every day of the Christian's calendar is marked
by the hand of God as a day of rejoicing."[16] When Napoleon was
sent to Elba, in proud defiance he adopted the motto *"Ubicunque
felix"* ("happy everywhere").[17] It was not true in his case; but the
Christian may be truly "happy everywhere" and always.

What Do You Treasure?

CHRISTIAN APOLOGIST RAVI ZACHARIAS writes in his book *Deliver
Us from Evil* about a fascinating experience that evidenced his
friend Sami's true values in life. The following account took place
while Ravi was visiting his friend in Beirut, Lebanon.

> One of Sami's great characteristics was fearlessness. One
> day he was driving with his wife along a highway on the out-
> skirts of Beirut when he suddenly saw a suitcase lying on the
> side of the road. Most people would not only have driven
> past it, they would have probably picked up speed, almost
> certain that it was booby-trapped. But not Sami. . . .
>
> Much against his wife's pleas, he stopped, walked over
> to the suitcase, and began to feel its contours.
>
> "Sami," she insisted, "leave it alone and let's go."
>
> She may as well have been talking to a blade of grass.
> Triumphantly, he shouted back to her, "Joy! I think it is full
> of something!"
>
> Hardly thrilled by that piece of information, Joy called to
> him once more to come away. But Sami was convinced that
> somebody had lost it. So, much to his wife's utter anguish,
> he brought it back to the car and took it home.
>
> To make a fascinating story short, when he opened it, he
> found every inch of space within crammed with money. It
> was certainly not the kind of experience that would cause
> one to moan in despair, "Why me, Lord?" Fortunately, there
> was also an address and telephone number inside, and after
> repeated attempts at phoning, someone finally answered.
> Sami asked for the person by name, and when, in a doleful

voice, the man identified himself, Sami asked him, "Sir, have you lost something?"

Taken aback, the man paused and then said, "Have you found it?"

The rest of the story was basically that of a frenzied effort on the part of the man to make arrangements to retrieve his suitcase, which he had lost en route to the boat he was to catch as he was attempting to leave the country.

I was in Sami's home when the owner of the suitcase brought his family to meet, in flesh and blood, a man with a soul in a disintegrating society. Beirut was once called the pearl of the Middle East. Its beauty was both proverbial and historic. Yet in the tangled web of human greed and ideological heartlessness, it is a city now where piles of rubble have taken the place of majestic buildings and ancient edifices. In this war-torn suburb a family was dumbfounded to see a life that had not been destroyed by the evil around it.

As they sat in Sami's living room, completely overwhelmed, Sami said gently, "You think you have recovered your treasure. Let me tell you how passing a treasure this is. With the fragile state of our country, this could become completely worthless overnight. Let me give you the greatest and most enduring treasure you can ever have."

Sami then handed the man a copy of the Bible. That was Ravi Zacharias's last glimpse of Beirut before he left for Cyprus that night. He said he had "witnessed the courage of a man who sought things that are eternal amid the ruins of human wickedness."[18]

Do you demonstrate godly values, true happiness, and internal peace? Perhaps one of the greatest evangelistic tools we have is the decision we make to evidence to a world that is empty, disillusioned, and without hope that our treasure is different and our attitude is one that rejoices in the Lord regardless of the circumstances. Our neighbors are watching us to see if we really have what we claim Christians uniquely possess. Like Sami, let those near you see that you are a person who seeks "things that are eternal amid the ruins of human wickedness."

⇒ TWO ⇐

Whose Kingdom Are
You Building?

Ashley Danielle Qubre had the unusual honor of speaking at the Mayoral Prayer Breakfast in Washington, D.C., when she was only ten years old. Among other things, she decided to speak about kingdoms, man's kingdom and God's kingdom.

Good morning, Mayor Barry, platform guests, ladies, and gentlemen. I appreciate this opportunity to speak to the leadership of the greatest city in the world on behalf of the children. I wondered what I would say to you when I was first asked if I would make a presentation. Being young limits the experience you have in most areas, but not in being a child.

Jesus said, "Unless you become like a child you cannot enter the kingdom." When I think about my friends, who are all young people like myself, many things come to mind.

If you would like to be a child in God's kingdom, I will share some of what we think about and do.

Children play together, have lots of fun, and sometimes fight, but the very next day we make up and play again. Wouldn't it be wonderful if mothers and fathers, sisters and brothers, neighbors and our leaders would be more that way? It hurts us when we see you fighting and not making up.

When you tell us something, we believe it, and we don't ask many questions. We have faith and trust in you until we grow up and find it's really not that way with adults. I think you tell us Bible stories because we are children. The Bible stories do us a lot of good, but you don't tell each other Bible stories. Are they only good for children?

You teach us that when we have a problem, we should talk it out with others and with Jesus. You say that we should pray about it and keep our hearts right for Jesus. You say that Jesus can solve all of our problems, both big and small. But we notice, when people get older and have problems, they are embarrassed to talk like that among themselves. We wonder if you really mean it, or is Jesus only for kids? I am still young enough to believe that Jesus knows how to solve my problems, the problems of the city, and of the world. I hope I never grow old enough to stop believing and that you all become like children in search of God's kingdom.

Thank you very much for listening to me. God bless you all![1]

Ashley is right. We adults sometimes do lose track of God's kingdom. In fact, for some reason, as we grow older and begin to succeed and accumulate stature, prestige, and material things, many decide to build their own *kingdoms*.

This notion isn't something that has occurred just during the twentieth century or the technological age. People have fantasized about becoming great and attaining power since the beginning of humankind. The exceptional athlete Deion Sanders thought that obtaining status, money, and power was the ultimate answer to finding peace. He is known as "Prime Time," the hottest defensive back in the National Football League and a base-stealing sensation in major league baseball. He is the only athlete in history to play in both a World Series and a Super Bowl. In the minds of many, he had it all. But Deion found that his possessions, financial security, and popularity didn't give him the satisfaction he thought they would. He said, "I tried everything. Parties, women, buying expensive jewelry and gadgets, and nothing helped. There was no peace. I was playing great, and every time I turned on the TV I could see myself on three or four commercials, but there was no peace, no joy, just emptiness inside."[2]

Deion had several friends who were concerned about his reckless lifestyle and his spiritual condition. They prayed for him and found times to talk to him about Christ. One night after an intensive emotional battle, Deion totally committed his life to Jesus Christ, and his life radically changed. He recently said, "Before I found Christ I had all the material comforts and all the money and all the fame and popularity, but I had no peace. When I found Christ, I found what I had been missing all those years. Only then was I able to trust in God's will for my life and, also, relax and trust Him for the outcome."[3]

Because Satan is the originator of false hope, empty satisfaction, and illusion, the struggle with pride, power, and position will continue until Jesus Christ banishes the enemy of our souls into the hell that has been created for him and his fallen angels.

I love the fact that the Bible doesn't try to cover up people's weaknesses, insecurities, or failures. From its beginning pages, we see an extreme case of sibling rivalry with Cain murdering his brother Abel. We read about person after person who, in many cases, would remind us of the front pages of our newspapers.

Adam had a blame-shifting problem.
Cain was given to violence and murder.
Noah had a drinking problem.
Amnon committed rape and incest.
Haman was a deceitful manipulator.
Jezebel was just plain mean.
Moses had a temper problem.
Abraham had a lying problem.
King Saul was consumed with jealousy.
David had a moral failure.
Sarah suffered from pessimism and laughed at God.
Jonah ran from God and wanted to die.
Thomas suffered from bouts of doubt.
Peter was impetuous, loud, and often rash.
Barak could rightly be called timid and cowardly.

Nadab and Abihu had an attitude problem when it came to
following God's instructions.
Gehazi struggled with an honesty problem.
Simon, in Acts, had a greed problem.[4]

For some reason, when I was a young Christian, I thought that
the people who would be used in the Bible as examples would
have everything under control. But God, in his sovereign wisdom,
used people who were very much like you and me. A classic sam-
ple of people—the twelve apostles—who seemingly should have
acted differently but didn't is found in the Gospel of Mark. It
seems that the apostles were overheard having a dispute one day
when they were walking. Jesus decided to quiz them about the
quarrel they were having. He asked them, "'What were you arguing about on the road?' But they kept quiet because on the way
they had argued about who was the greatest" (Mark 9:33–34).
These guys may have been competitors, measuring themselves
against themselves, comparing their abilities, achievements, and
talents against one another. Perhaps they were trying to determine
which one(s) would be Jesus' favorite(s).

They not only argued about who was the greatest, but also
may have been territorial. Perhaps they didn't want anyone invad-
ing their turf, or maybe each thought he was the only one who
could be used by God and that no one else could measure up.

"Teacher," said John, "we saw a man driving out demons
in your name and we told him to stop, because he was not
one of us."
"Do not stop him," Jesus said. "No one who does a miracle in my name can in the next moment say anything bad about
me, for whoever is not against us is for us" (Mark 9:38–40).

God's kingdom is different from any personal kingdom we
could build. It is very different from the kingdoms we see governments, systems, corporations, or politicians build. The rules of
God's kingdom are perfect and represent absolute truth. They
have eternal value and reward.

Even though the apostles had Jesus as their teacher, before his resurrection and ascension and the day of Pentecost, they did not fully understand the kingdom they were part of. On one occasion Jesus explained to his followers the principles of becoming great *in God's kingdom.*

> Then James and John, the sons of Zebedee, came to him. "Teacher," they said, "we want you to do for us whatever we ask."
>
> "What do you want me to do for you?" he asked.
>
> They replied, "Let one of us sit at your right and the other at your left in your glory."
>
> "You don't know what you are asking," Jesus said. "Can you drink the cup I drink or be baptized with the baptism I am baptized with?"
>
> "We can," they answered.
>
> Jesus said to them, "You will drink the cup I drink and be baptized with the baptism I am baptized with, but to sit at my right or left is not for me to grant. These places belong to those for whom they have been prepared."
>
> When the ten heard about this, they became indignant with James and John. Jesus called them together and said, "You know that those who are regarded as rulers of the Gentiles lord it over them, and their high officials exercise authority over them. Not so with you. Instead, whoever wants to become great among you must be your servant, and whoever wants to be first must be slave of all. For even the Son of Man did not come to be served, but to serve, and to give his life as a ransom for many" (Mark 10:35–45).

On the road to Jerusalem, Jesus told his disciples that he was about to suffer and be killed. He knew that in God's plan suffering precedes glory, the cross comes before the crown, and true greatness is achieved by serving rather than being served. The disciples missed what Jesus was saying. They were preoccupied with their own little kingdoms: Who would be the greatest? Who would sit at Jesus' right or left hand? How many followers would they have?

Many people in today's world have concerns similar to those of James and John. They are more driven than ever, climbing the corporate ladder, pursuing an upwardly mobile lifestyle, managing their financial portfolios, achieving public recognition as speakers, authors, musicians, and political figures. But as they are expending all this energy, time, and talent, one crucial question must be asked: Whose kingdom are they building?

Jesus used this occasion to remind his disciples of three eternal principles that still apply to us today. *Sovereignty* operates in all of our lives, *suffering* is necessary for spiritual growth, and *servanthood* is a sign of spiritual maturity and is necessary for every leader in God's kingdom.

Sovereignty

I HAVE TRIED NOT to complicate this attribute of God in my life with heavy theological terms or concepts. To understand the sovereignty of God is to realize that God is God and that he can do anything he desires, whenever he wishes, to whomever he wants. To me this means that because I love the Lord with all of my heart, he will lead me to do his will, place me in any geographical location, or give me any responsibility that he wishes. He will also determine what is best for me as I grow more Christlike.

David wrote, "The LORD has established his throne in heaven, and his kingdom rules over all" (Ps. 103:19). Daniel identifies God as the "Most High" (Dan. 4:17, 25, 34) and reminds us that "the Most High God is sovereign over the kingdoms of men and sets over them anyone he wishes" (Dan. 5:21). Paul wrote to Timothy that God is the "blessed and only Ruler, the King of kings and Lord of lords" (1 Tim. 6:15). He also reminded the Ephesian believers that God "works out everything in conformity with the purpose of his will" (Eph. 1:11). Thus, *The Concise Evangelical Dictionary of Theology* is correct in defining sovereignty by saying, "The sovereignty of God ... expresses the very nature of God

as all-powerful and omnipotent, able to accomplish his good pleasure, carry out his decreed will, and keep his promises."[5]

We cannot only declare that "Jesus is Lord" because he is, but
we can have the personal assurance of knowing that Jesus is Lord
of our lives and knows what is best for us, and that he intervenes
in our lives and has everything under control. Abraham Lincoln
said, "That the Almighty does make use of human agencies and
directly intervenes in human affairs is one of the plainest statements in the Bible. I have had so many evidences of His direction, so many instances when I have been controlled by some
other power than my own will, that I cannot doubt that this power
comes from above."[6]

Some have confused our human responsibility with God's sovereignty by thinking, "If God is controlling everything, then why
worry about our choices? God's going to do it anyway." F. H.
Klooster explains, "Divine sovereignty and human responsibility
are paradoxical and beyond human comprehension, but not contradictory. Divine sovereignty and human sovereignty are certainly
contradictory, but divine sovereignty and human responsibility are
not. God uses human means in history to accomplish his purposes,
yet such means do not involve coercion."[7]

Great comfort comes from understanding that God is sover-
eignly involved in our lives and that he is building his kingdom
through us. As his children we can know that his thoughts are
about us, his eye is on us, and his hand guides us as we walk life's
journey. In his classic book *Spiritual Leadership,* J. Oswald
Sanders said:

> Spiritual leaders are not made by election or appointment,
> by men or any combination of men, nor by conferences or
> synods. Only God can make them. Simply holding a position
> of importance does not constitute one as a leader, nor does
> taking courses in leadership or resolving to become a leader.
> The only method is that of qualifying to be a leader. Reli-
> gious position can be conferred by bishops and boards, but
> not spiritual authority, which is the prime essential of Chris-

tian leadership. That comes—often unsought—to those who in earlier life have proved themselves worthy of it by spirituality, discipline, ability, and diligence, men who have heeded the command: "Do you seek great things for yourself? Do not seek them," and instead have sought first the kingdom of God. Spiritual leadership is a thing of the Spirit and is conferred by God alone.[8]

Jesus did not rebuke James and John because they desired to become great in God's kingdom; he only reminded them that God's sovereignty is involved in these kinds of decisions. He said, "These places belong to those for whom they have been prepared" (Mark 10:40). In other words, preparation for future responsibility is continually going on in our lives, and God is involved in stationing certain people in certain places for specific responsibilities in his kingdom. Paul reminded the leaders of the church in Ephesus that the "Holy Spirit has made you overseers" (Acts 20:28). God gave them the position of leadership in that church. Jeremiah tells us that the word of the Lord came to him saying:

"Before I formed you in the womb I knew you,
     before you were born I set you apart;
     I appointed you as a prophet to the nations." (Jer. 1:5)

DAVID REALIZED:

All the days ordained for me
     were written in your book
     before one of them came to be. (Ps. 139:16)

God's sovereignty governs our lives. Understanding this truth will help us to be less worried about what comes next and to rest in God's will. It should not keep us from doing our best or from being diligent in our effort to reach our potential, but as we discipline our lives and grow in our understanding of his will, we can be assured that he will direct us in all our ways. Some might interpret this attitude as a "cop-out" or as escapism in the way Christians look at life. This is not true. Understanding God's sovereignty in our lives is simply the first step in looking at life from God's vantage point. Warren Wiersbe said, "Many people think that a 'spiritual Christian' is mystical, dreamy, impractical, and distant. When he prays, he shifts his voice into a sepulchral tone in tremolo. This kind of unctuous piety is a poor example of true spirituality. To be 'spiritually minded' simply means to look at earth from heaven's point of view. The spiritually minded believer makes his decisions on the basis of eternal values and not the passing fads of society."[9] This person is concerned about building God's kingdom, not a kingdom of his or her own.

Christians who trust God in every area of their lives present a tremendous witness. How complicated life is to the person without Christ. Going through life's storms without the peace of God must be unsettling, to say the least. A friend of mine who is a car salesman told me recently of an experience he had when he delivered a beautiful automobile to an extremely wealthy person. The man's home and grounds were breathtaking. The car dealer knew a little about the wealth of the individual and that his business was on the increase. Nevertheless, the dealer told me, "Tom, this person was so unhappy, he looked empty." Scores of times I have said to myself in similar instances, "This person thought that position, wealth, education, prestige, or the accumulation of things would bring him or her happiness and a sense of fulfillment, but only knowing Christ can do that."

Demonstrating our trust for God is critical in this chaotic world. When others watch our lives—whether we have great wealth or are poor, are involved in leadership or serve in humble ways—and see the kind of fulfillment we have, they will be drawn to the Christian faith.

Suffering

JESUS ALSO TAUGHT HIS disciples that spiritual leadership involves suffering. Many do not understand this principle. In his book *The Jesus I Never Knew,* Philip Yancey quoted a British psychologist as saying to the Royal Society of Medicine:

The spirit of self-sacrifice which permeates Christianity, and is so highly prized in the Christian religious life, is masochism moderately indulged. A much stronger expression of it is to be found in Christ's teaching in the Sermon on the Mount. This blesses the poor, the meek, the persecuted; exhorts us not to resist evil but to offer the second cheek to the sinner; and to do good to them that hate you and forgive men their trespasses. All this breathes masochism.[10]

This psychologist is not unlike many today who do not understand that suffering is part of every life and that tremendous growth occurs in the process. He completely misses what Jesus was communicating to his listeners.

Just as we are to understand that God is sovereign over our lives, so we are to understand that there is a price to pay for leadership. Suffering can encourage spiritual growth that prepares us for greater responsibility in God's kingdom. Jesus asked James and John, "Can you drink the cup I drink or be baptized with the baptism I am baptized with?" (Mark 10:38). In his commentary on Mark, William Barclay describes these two Jewish metaphors.

It was the custom at a royal banquet for the king to hand the cup to his guests. The cup therefore became a metaphor for the life and experience that God handed out to men. "My cup overflows," said the Psalmist (Psalm 23:5) when he spoke of a life and experience of happiness given to him by God. "In the hand of the LORD there is a cup," said the Psalmist (Psalm 75:8) when he was thinking of the fate in store for the wicked and the disobedient. Isaiah, thinking of the disasters which had come upon the people of Israel, describes them as having drunk "at the hand of the LORD the cup of his wrath" (Isa. 51:17). The cup speaks of the experience allotted to men by God.[11]

Jesus also spoke of "the baptism I am baptized with" (Mark 10:39). Again, Barclay comments:

The Greek verb *baptizein* means to dip. Its past participle (*bebaptismenos*) means submerged, and it is regularly used of being *submerged* in any experience.... The expression, as Jesus used it here, had nothing to do with technical baptism. What he is saying is, "Can you bear to go through the terrible experience which I have to go through? Can you face being submerged in hatred and pain and death, as I have to be?" He was telling these two disciples that without a cross there can never be a crown.[12]

James and John did not understand the depth of the question Jesus asked them. They had not thought it through but merely wanted the prize of leadership without paying the price. Their response was "We can" (Mark 10:39). Today they might have responded, "Not a problem; we can do that. Piece of cake! Just let us know what we need to do to become great!" They didn't realize the degree of suffering they would endure as they became leaders in God's kingdom.

Jesus knew that James and John and the other apostles would suffer in their lives. James became the first apostolic martyr when he was beheaded by Herod Agrippa (Acts 12:2). When he placed his neck on Herod's bloody chopping block and as the sharp ax was lifted above his head, I wonder if James thought of Jesus' question, "Can you drink the cup I drink?"

When John was imprisoned on the island of Patmos because of his faith, I wonder if he thought back to the day, decades earlier, when Jesus asked, "Are you able to be baptized with the baptism I am baptized with?" Oswald Chambers said, "We all know people who have been made much meaner and more irritable and more intolerable to live with by suffering; it is not right to say that all suffering perfects. It only perfects one type of person—the one who accepts the call of God in Christ Jesus."[13] If we want to become great in God's kingdom, we may have to take part in the postgraduate school of suffering. Leo Tolstoy said, "It is by those who have suffered that the world has been advanced."[14] Similarly, Chuck Swindoll said, "God's wisest saints are often people who endure pain rather than escape it."[15]

Many leaders are unwilling to pay the price for leadership. This could be the reason why leadership in the political and, sadly, the religious world is going through a loss of respect. Patterson and Kim report in *The Day America Told the Truth:*

> Our leaders are still giving advice, but we are not listening. America's leadership no longer leads anyone.
>
> We asked people to give letter grades of A to F to leaders in four categories: religion, politics, business, and education.
>
> The highest grade that any kind of leader got was a C+ for religion. All of the others got low Cs or even a grade of D. C- was the combined grade average for leadership in America!
>
> Why? One reason is because they have lied to us—over and over and over. Our leaders have told the most bold-faced lies.
>
> So who are our moral leaders now? Well, the overwhelming majority of people (93 percent) said that they—and nobody else—determine what is and what isn't moral in their lives. They base their decisions on their own experience, even on their daily whims.
>
> In addition, almost as large a majority confessed that they would violate the established rules of their religion (84 percent), or that they had actually violated a law because they thought that it was wrong in their view (81 percent).
>
> We are a law unto ourselves.
> We have made ourselves the authority over church and God.
> We have made ourselves the clear authority over the government.
> We have made ourselves the authority over laws and the police.
> ... There are important implications that follow from all of this. For example, most of us are not prepared—as so many others were in earlier generations—to sacrifice our lives for our country. Or for anything else, it seems.

When we asked what beliefs people would die for, the answer for almost half (48 percent) was "None."

Here is the measure of Americans' alienation from the traditional authority of God and country.

Fewer than one in three (30 percent) would be willing to die for God and religion under any circumstances.

Even fewer (24 percent) would die for their country.[16]

This sad commentary should remind us that people are looking for examples of truth, righteousness, and stability. I believe that when they see it in our Christian lives, they will listen and hunger for what we have.

When people see us suffer through the trials of life, they will notice a difference in how we react. Joni Eareckson Tada, who was paralyzed in a tragic diving accident, said, "The way you and I handle our big and little trials makes the world pause in its frantic, headlong pursuits. Our godly response to those obstacles and perplexities in our lives literally kicks the psychological crutches right out from under the skeptic. The unbeliever can no longer refuse to face the reality of our faith."[17]

To build any corporation, business, or "kingdom" takes tremendous discipline. To build God's kingdom takes sacrifice, determination to grow through suffering, and a commitment to be the greatest servant we can become to our Creator God.

Servanthood

"YOU KNOW THAT THOSE who are regarded as rulers of the Gentiles lord it over them, and their high officials exercise authority over them. Not so with you. Instead, whoever wants to become great among you must be your servant, and whoever wants to be first must be slave of all" (Mark 10:42–44).

The way to maturity and leadership in the kingdom of God is the road of servanthood. Even Albert Einstein said, "It is high time that the ideal of success should be replaced by the ideal of service."[18]

As we serve Christ with a life of obedience, we cannot respond to life as those without Christ do. Malcolm Muggeridge said:

> The world's way of responding to intimations of decay is to engage equally in idiot hopes and idiot despair. On the one hand some new policy or discovery is confidently expected to put everything to rights: a new fuel, a new drug, détente, world government. On the other, some disaster is as confidently expected to prove our undoing. Capitalism will break down. Fuel will run out. Plutonium will lay us low. Atomic waste will kill us off. Overpopulation will suffocate us, or alternatively, a declining birth rate will put us more surely at the mercy of our enemies.
>
> In Christian terms, such hopes and fears are equally beside the point. As Christians we know that in this world we have no continuing city, that crowns roll in the dust and that every earthly kingdom must sometime flounder. We acknowledge a King men did not crown and cannot dethrone, and we are citizens of a city of God they did not build and cannot destroy. Thus, the apostle Paul wrote to the Christians in Rome, living in a society as depraved and dissolute as our own. Paul exhorted them to be steadfast, unmovable, always abounding in God's work, to concern themselves with the things that are unseen, for the things which are seen are temporal but the things that are not seen are eternal. It was in the breakdown of Rome that Christendom was born. Now in the breakdown of Christendom there are the same requirements and the same possibilities to eschew the fantasy of a disintegrating world, and seek the reality of what is not seen and eternal, the reality of Christ.[19]

Servanthood is the way of God's kingdom. Somehow we must be content to be servants. If God chooses us to be leaders that have tremendous responsibilities, or if he chooses us to serve behind the lines where we seldom are recognized, our attitude should remain the same. We are servants of the Most High God.

Any role or responsibility he chooses for us is perfect . . . because he always knows what is best, and in a sense, we have been created for "such a time as this."

The inscription in the Stanford University Chapel says, "The highest service may be prepared for and done in the humblest surroundings. In silence, in waiting, in obscure, unnoticed offices, in years of uneventful, unrecorded duties, the Son of God grew and waxed strong."[20]

Leadership is a subject that we hear much about. Some people go about leading like a "bull in a china closet." This style of leadership will never attract people to God's kingdom. But if we truly live, lead, and treat people as Jesus instructed his disciples that day on the road to Jerusalem, then like them our spiritually hungry world will want the Christ we have.

"'I have set you an example that you should do as I have done for you. I tell you the truth, no servant is greater than his master, nor is a messenger greater than the one who sent him. Now that you know these things, you will be blessed if you do them'" (John 13:15–17).

⇒ THREE ⇐

Who Sets Your Agenda?

SIX-MONTH-OLD BILLY HALL LAY in bed with a fever that would not break. Where he lived, in Upper Volta (Burkina Faso), East Africa, there was little his missionary parents could do for him. They prayed and sought the best help available, but his condition only worsened.

Day and night the Africans would peer in the windows and stand around the door of John and Cuba Hall's meager hut. Among themselves the villagers kept asking, "What will the missionaries do if their boy dies? Will they conclude that their God has failed them and leave us?" The Halls had bonded with the Mosi people, yet the tribal people knew that this kind of grief could persuade the young couple to return home or relocate to a part of the world that had more comfort and better protection from deadly illnesses.

Billy's breath became more labored, and he simply could not struggle any longer. His little chest stopped moving as his heart ceased beating. At six months of age Billy was dead. John and Cuba could not figure it out. They had all the normal thoughts and emotions of grieving parents who had lost a child. "Why Billy? How could this happen to us? We were being faithful to the call of God."

At that time, John and Cuba could not have understood how the people of Ouagaudougou curiously and intensely watched them. Their every move was being registered in the hearts and minds of the Mosi people.

Within hours of Billy's death the Halls buried him. Understandably, their grief was the most painful experience they had ever gone through, but they quickly decided that they would stay and continue the work God had called them to do. They were determined to translate the Mosi Bible into the Mori language, a language that had never been put into writing.

John and Cuba had both originally gone out as single missionaries and vigorously studied and learned Mori, the language of the Mosi people. As their excitement grew toward working with people who had little understanding of Jesus Christ or the Bible, they also fell in love with each other and decided to become married. The African people were touched when John and Cuba had their ceremony performed in both Mori and English. The people were also thrilled when Cuba became pregnant and when little Billy was born. The bond between the Mosi people and the Halls could have been broken and life would have gone on if John and Cuba had decided to leave because of their private pain. Perhaps their deep grief reminded them of the spiritual void in the lives of those in the village, or perhaps Billy's death made them more determined to offer "life" to the Africans—for whatever reason, they chose to stay.

The Halls remained in Ouagaudougou for thirty years, and during that time they translated most of the Mosi Bible into the Mori language. The fruit of their life's work is remarkable. Countless Mosi people understand the love of God and his eternal Word because of the Halls' faithfulness. It would have been easier for them to return to the comforts of the States, but they had a deep inner conviction that the God who created them had plans for them to stay. Their destiny was to work with the Mosi people. No one and nothing—not even the death of their precious Billy— could deter them from doing God's will. Looking back, the Halls understood that the death of their son was the event that opened the door for the rest of their ministry with the Mosi people, for a bond formed through pain is difficult to break. When evaluating their years of service in Africa, one has to come to the conclusion that they did a tremendous job and set an uncompromising example. The Halls let God set their agenda and continued to trust him with their lives.

Who determines your agenda? I'm not necessarily talking about your "to do" list around the house or the schedule you are required to follow at work. The question goes deeper than that. Who or what helps you determine the direction you take in life? Who or what *owns* you?

You might say, "I determine my destiny. I own me." Many respond that way, but the Bible teaches that "Many are the plans in a man's heart, but it is the LORD's purpose that prevails" (Prov. 19:21). The God who created you has a purpose for your life. You can choose to plan your own life or determine to walk in the purpose God has for you. Again, the writer of Proverbs says:

> Listen to my instruction and be wise;
> > do not ignore it.
> Blessed is the man who listens to me,
> > watching daily at my doors,
> > waiting at my doorway,
> For whoever finds me, finds life
> > and receives favor from the Lord.
> But whoever fails to find me harms himself;
> > all who hate me love death. (Prov. 8:33–36)

Lee McFarland is another example of someone who decided he had a different career call in life. His colleagues were shocked when they learned that he was going to leave his job as the director of hardware manufacturing for the Microsoft Corporation of Seattle, which would soon have made him a millionaire. He wasn't leaving for the typical reasons—bigger company, better job, easier climb up the executive ladder. He felt that God wanted him to become a minister. His agenda had radically changed.

Lee said, "I had found my ultimate job. When I left my position at Microsoft, one of the guys said, 'You're a minister now? Are you crazy!'"

Lee's not crazy; he's fulfilled. He's not accumulating the wealth he would have in his Microsoft career, but he has the peace and contentment that no amount of money could buy. Today you will find Lee in a city in Arizona serving as pastor of a unique and fast-growing church.

I recently telephoned Lee and asked him if he regretted his decision. He began to silently weep with gratitude as he described how the church that was started only fifteen months ago was now running over three hundred people. He said, "The marriages that have been restored, and the people who have found meaning in life are more than any job could pay. I don't regret the loss of income or benefits; I'm accumulating wealth in heaven." By the way, Lee mentioned to me that he paid more in taxes in his last year with Microsoft than he made the entire next year.

Do you know God's agenda for you? He created you for a purpose, and you have a divine destiny. He has uniquely gifted you and desires to use you in his kingdom. The Halls' commitment to literally move to the ends of the earth and stay as long as God wanted them to and Lee's decision to walk away from a lucrative career are examples of how God plucks people from college classrooms and corporate boardrooms to become involved in careers that could be very different from what they thought they would do in life. Even more significant, however, is that the Holy Spirit who dwells in every believer is constantly, gently challenging and at times intensely convicting us to live every day according to God's agenda. Not only is God interested in our career moves; he is also interested in the way we live and how we treat others.

The Holy Spirit helps us as committed followers of Jesus Christ to act in ways that are consistent with our new nature. Thus, peer pressure, or doing something because "the crowd is doing it," should be far less significant in our lives. Culture or fads should move us less and less as we grow in Christ. When we act according to a current fad of behavior, or are easily moved—or moved at all—to live like the worldly system, non-Christians will naturally wonder who is directing our lives and will question whether Christianity really has power to change a life.

Compromise or Commitment?

IN *THE ANNALS OF the American Academy of Political and Social Sciences* (July 1998), Mark A. Shibley reported,

> American Protestant evangelicals, on the move during the past third of a century, somehow acquired a reputation for being world-denying. Many who observed their role in the new Christian Right those years overlooked other changes, including moves toward world-affirmation.... *The conclusion that the most important feat of contemporary American evangelicalism is its transformation into a world-affirming faith.* He cites evangelical leaders who, contrary to what their ancestors taught, urge followers *to be at ease in the world.* The distinctive worship styles reflect secular influences.
>
> Most evangelicals are not influenced by secular feminists, but their lifestyles have changed thanks to domestic upheavals in post industrial America; gender roles and hierarchies have changed.
>
> The new organizational forms of evangelicalism borrow from market and mall—hardly otherworldly places. Some even speak of their churches as businesses. And the new Christian Right itself is in the business of offering worldly and world-affirming outcomes. Most of all, many evangelicals now preach prosperity and thrive on signs of it. They have assets. *Being born-again can be profoundly life transforming. Their churches facilitate self-transcendence—the experience of the sacred.* Their churches provide identity to seekers.
>
> What's ahead? *Evangelicalism will continue to flourish in culturally current forms.* Drinking, dancing, and divorce—old shibboleths—serve that function less and less, as more born-again Christians are involved in all three. American Protestant evangelicals are not necessarily turning secular, but, *sociologically speaking, it is impossible to be in the world and not of the world,* despite evangelical efforts (italics added).[1]

The church in America could lose its cutting edge on evangelizing this country as well as its powerful influence in reaching the world

at large. Why? Because when we compromise our standards of righteousness and a godly lifestyle and begin to feel more comfortable in
this world, we are in great danger of losing God's blessing.

Perhaps more than any other nation before us, America has
the distinction of leading in world evangelism and missions
endeavors.[2] Yet church growth in this country is at a standstill and
denomination after denomination is declining in numbers. Many
are willing to give up God's decrees, and America is no longer
known as a country in revival. Although there are pockets of
revival in America, as a nation America is in trouble, because
God's Word warns us not to compromise with the world.

When we decide that the Bible is no longer inerrant, we have
a problem. When we determine that saving the lives of whales and
owls are of higher priority than saving the lives of unborn babies,
we have a problem. When we come to the conclusion that the
elderly and the weak should be allowed to end their lives pre-
maturely, we have a problem. When we decide that homosexuality is just an alternative lifestyle and is not sin, we have a problem.
When we consider ordaining homosexuals and lesbians as ministers in the Christian church, we have a problem. When we do or
even watch things that we know God would not approve of, we
have a problem.

Why? Because there is no way the *Holy* Spirit would be the
director, encourager, or motivator of such inconsistencies.
Remember this. If our friends, neighbors, or relatives see little or
no difference in the way we think and live, why would they want
what we have any more than they would want the New Age
agenda? Possibly the greatest attraction to the Christian faith is
the power of Jesus Christ to radically change lives and keep his
followers pure. If we choose to compromise, our influence fades
dramatically. A church full of worldly minded Christians is little
more than a club like the YMCA, YWCA, or Rotary. It is
absolutely imperative that communities see a church that is alive
in Christ; full of caring, loving, dedicated, compassionate people.
This type of church will draw people into its doors.

All of us can choose to look out for our own interests and organize our lives so that little thought is given to what the Lord would want us to do or what his will would be for a particular decision or what his agenda would be for our lives. Paul said about his young friend Timothy, "I have no one else like him, who takes a genuine interest in your welfare. For everyone looks out for his own interests, not those of Jesus Christ" (Phil. 2:20–21). As we walk life's journey, we can know that God wants to walk with us every day and help us know what to do in our difficult times as well as when things are going well.

Can we find God's agenda for our lives, whether it be a small decision or a career change like Lee's move from Microsoft? Can we know that the God who created us wants to be involved in our decisions? We *can* know. We are his children, and he desires to be intimately involved in the direction our lives are taking. It is not a difficult nor complicated task to know God's will. Scripture gives us several ideas about how to determine it. Permit me to share a formula that I have found helpful. I call it the 3 + 3 + 3 formula— nine principles that help to determine God's will for our lives.

The Principles of Divine Will

1. God has a will for our lives; choose to find his will.

It would be tremendous if every Christian would embrace the truth that God has a plan for his or her life. We are not here by chance or accident. From the moment of our conception, God was involved. Jeremiah said, "Before you were born I set you apart" (1:5). Isaiah said, "This is what the LORD says—your Redeemer, who formed you in the womb" (44:24). David said:

> If the LORD delights in a man's way,
>   he makes his steps firm;
> though he stumble, he will not fall,
>   for the LORD upholds him with his hand. (Ps. 37:23–24)

Great comfort comes from knowing that God has a perfect will for our lives. Such knowledge helps us rest in the assurance that he always knows what we are going through and has everything under control. The alternative is that we will trust in the fate of this world's system. That is frightening, because this world can be harsh, cruel, and unforgiving.

About sixty years after the book of Revelation was written, Polycarp served as the bishop of Smyrna. In A.D. 155 the old saint faced a decision that he had never experienced before. He was staying in an old farmhouse outside the city when his captors came for him. He knew that unless things had drastically changed, death awaited him because of his unswerving commitment to Christ. It is said that when his enemies arrived to seize him, he asked for permission to pray. They granted him this request, and Polycarp spoke to his heavenly Father for two hours.

In the city, the chief of the municipal police repeatedly asked him, "What harm is there in saying, Caesar is Lord?"

Polycarp answered him, "I am a Christian; if you would like to learn the Christian doctrine, appoint a day and let me speak."

Polycarp was threatened over and over again to be thrown to the wild animals or to be burned alive at the stake. The proconsul told him, "Swear the oath, and I will release you; curse the Christ."

His response was, "For four score and six years have I been his servant, and he has done me no wrong; how then can I blaspheme the King who saved me?" Frustrated and angry the proconsul sentenced the bishop to be burned to death at the stake.

It was customary to nail a person to the stake because the incredible pain of burning might make a person try to get away. Polycarp refused to be nailed to it, saying, "He who has granted me the strength to endure the fire will also grant me the grace to remain at the stake without moving." Until the flames took his last breath, he stood at the stake praying to the God who set the agenda for everything Polycarp did.[3]

In spite of his persecution, Polycarp knew that he was God's child and that his life was in God's hands. He probably never doubted that his Father was in control even at Polycarp's death.

The comfort that comes because we know that God has a perfect will for our lives helps us to be content in any situation. I've met numerous Christians on the brink of death, some who have gone through incredible tragedy or heartache, who have a peace that most in the world do not understand. Like Polycarp, they rest in the Lord and would not compromise their faith for anything— even another chance at life.

2. God wants to show us his will; choose to watch.

The writer of Hebrews prays, "May the God of peace ... equip you with everything good for doing his will" (Heb. 13:20–21). Every day, in every decision, we can know that God will direct us to do what is pleasing to him. We can choose to disobey him and do something that is wrong and sinful; however, if we are sensitive to the Holy Spirit who lives in us, we will know when we are in danger and about to compromise or where we have gone wrong and what we must do to make it right. Paul tells us to do "the will of God from your heart" (Eph. 6:6). God would never ask us to be concerned about doing his will if he didn't plan on clearly showing it to us.

3. Spiritual food is to do the will of God; choose to hunger for his will.

Jesus was passionate about doing his Father's will. He said, "The one who sent me is with me; he has not left me alone, for I always do what pleases him" (John 8:29). Centuries earlier the psalmist had said, "Let me live that I may praise you, and may your laws sustain me" (Ps. 119:175).

If we hunger and thirst to know the will of God and find a way to quiet our lives to listen to his Holy Spirit, then he will clearly show us the way we should go. Writer and theologian Paul Little said, "I was frustrated out of my mind trying to figure out the will of God. I was doing everything but getting into the presence of God and asking Him to show me."[4]

The Principles of Divine Obedience

4. God knows everything about us; choose to commit your past, present, and future to him.

As Christians, we no longer belong to ourselves. We have been bought with a price (1 Cor. 7:23). The sale of our lives has been closed. David instructs, "Commit your way to the LORD; trust in him" (Ps. 37:5). Our attitude must be, "Lord, it really doesn't matter what I want. It's your will that I desire." Doing the will of God will always give us a sense of fulfillment and assurance that we have been obedient to our Creator.

For years the Harlem Globetrotter basketball star Meadowlark Lemon lived a life of doing his own thing. He said:

> "I grew up in Wilmington, North Carolina. My parents divorced when I was very young. Part of the time I lived with my aunt and grandmother. My dad lived just down the street from them, so I could visit him anytime. I often spent summers in New York with my mother.
>
> "Growing up, I was not in church. The only times I went were Christmas and Easter. I thought God was some kind of surreal thing that we prayed to when we got in trouble and He beat up on us when we messed up.
>
> "Fifteen years ago I was in Hollywood, California. I was ready to party. One day, I picked up a telephone book in my home and God spoke to me. I had no Christian background, but I knew something was happening. It was almost as if God was physically touching me. He told me to call Heidi.
>
> "Heidi was a Jewish girl who made costumes for actors in Hollywood. She also was a Christian. Well, I went to Heidi's fashion design studio, and at the same time God sent a young preacher to Heidi's. When he arrived, he told her, 'Heidi, I never come here. I don't know why I am here today, but I do know I have to be here today.'

"As I walked through the door, Heidi said, 'You need Jesus.' Together, the preacher and Heidi shared the gospel with me and then led me in the sinner's prayer. After I said it, I thought there might be flashing lights and sirens. But there wasn't. Later I realized that God had cleaned me up on the inside. After about six months I started sharing my testimony."

Today you might see Meadowlark on a Christian television program sharing his testimony. His new passion in life is to be obedient to the Lord and lead as many people to Christ as he can. He often speaks to young people in schools about the dangers of drugs and alcohol, saying, "There is only one way to be delivered from an addiction—through Jesus. Jesus said, 'Seek ye first the kingdom of God, and his righteousness; and all these things shall be added unto you' (Matt. 6:33)." He adds, "When you're sick, you seek Jesus, because He's the Great Physician. Likewise, if you have an addiction, seek Jesus. Some are healed immediately. For others it takes time."

Meadowlark's conviction is, "God does not play games. He wants you to give Him everything that you have—your whole life."[5]

Meadowlark no longer owns himself. He made the most important choice in his life when he gave God his past, present, and future. Because of that decision, he is more fulfilled today than ever before.

5. God is trustworthy; choose to rely on him.

Many Christians spend little time asking God for his will. Instead, they try to control their own lives without trusting God. Sometimes people fear that God will not listen to their prayers or that God is angry with them for one reason or another. This fear could come from growing up in an unusually harsh home or having hurtful experiences that result in a misunderstanding of what God is like. God is not a harsh God, nor will he mistreat us in any way. King Solomon said to

> trust in the LORD with all your heart
> > and lean not on your own understanding;
> in all your ways acknowledge him,
> > and he will make your paths straight. (Prov. 3:5–6)

We need never fear God's will, for he can be trusted absolutely. G. Christian Weiss asks: Can you think of a father who has no will or plan for the life of the son? Can you imagine a mother who has no clear will or definite ambition for her daughter? Can you imagine a man who has no special desire or pattern in the one he chooses to be his wife? Can you conceive of a king or ruler who has no will or desire or law to govern the conduct of his people? A captain who has no plan for his soldiery? An employer who has no plan or pattern to guide the labor of his workers? If so, then you may also think that God does not have a plan for your life, for every one of these symbols is used in the Bible to represent the relation the Christian bears to his Lord.[6]

6. Regardless of your feelings, choose to be obedient.

Many times I have talked with Christians who emotionally do not "feel" like being obedient to God's will. I have talked to Christians who want to get divorced because they do not "feel" that they love their spouses any longer. I have met with believers who do not "feel" like attending church, praying, or reading their Bibles, so they stop these critical disciplines. At times we "feel" like doing the wrong thing more than we feel like doing the right thing; however, we need to be obedient to what we know is right no matter what our emotions are telling us.

Some think that we should listen to our emotions in determining what we should do. That is like the tail wagging the dog. If we go through life making decisions because we emotionally feel like doing this or that, we will have lives of inconsistency. Though God created us to have emotions, and we can enjoy these feelings, we must remember that our emotions can lie to us and confuse us. We might emotionally feel something because of the amount of sleep we had the night before or because of what we ate for dinner. We could be tired, burnt out, or have a lot on our mind. Many things contribute to how we feel. We must learn to do what we *know* is right by faith and what we understand God's will to be no matter how we feel.

Joseph (Gen. 37–41) likely felt misunderstood and mistreated and possibly wondered if God knew what was going on in his life. He was sold into slavery because his brothers rejected him (almost killed him) because they didn't want him in the family any longer.

Potiphar, an Egyptian official, purchased Joseph to be his slave. As a slave, Joseph was blessed in all he did because God was with him. Potiphar's wife lusted after Joseph and attempted to have an affair with him, but Joseph refused her adulterous attempts by saying, "How then could I do such a wicked thing and sin against God?" (Gen. 39:9). Because she literally tried to entrap him when they were alone in Potiphar's home, he bolted from her grip leaving his coat in her hand. Probably because she had been rejected, she accused him of rape. When her husband heard his wife's accusation of Joseph, he became furious and put Joseph into prison.

Can you imagine how you would feel if you were in Joseph's place? First, your siblings hate and reject you. You are living in a different country and are forced to work for someone as a slave. You are trying to make the best of it when your owner's spouse tries to commit adultery with you. Since this goes against everything you believe, you reject that person's advances only to find that you are accused of rape. Joseph might have wondered, "What in the world is going on? I am doing my best to be obedient in spite of my circumstances, but things keep getting turned upside down."

If Joseph had negative thoughts and said negative words, the Bible doesn't give them. When Joseph was in prison God blessed him. The prisoners began to respect him for his wisdom and ability to interpret dreams. One day Pharaoh had a dream, and one of his servants knew that Joseph had the gift of interpreting dreams. Pharaoh called for him, and with great detail Joseph interpreted

Pharaoh's dream. Pharaoh also noticed Joseph's unusual wisdom and ability. As a result, he promoted Joseph to the number two position in the country of Egypt. In that position Joseph was used by God to save hundreds of thousands of people from starvation—including the lives of his own father and brothers—during a famine.

The circumstances in Joseph's life looked bad for many years. Nevertheless, he decided to trust God and be obedient to God's will despite his circumstances. Deep down inside he knew that God was in control.

When Joseph's brothers found out that he was now a very high official in the government and could have punished them for the way they treated him years before, they were frightened. Joseph said to them, "Do not be distressed and do not be angry with yourselves for selling me here, because it was to save lives that God sent me ahead of you" (Gen. 45:5).

You may not understand what is going on in your life. Don't try so hard to understand the events, but rather try to understand that because of your sincere love for God, he will accomplish his will in your life. Be obedient to God no matter how you feel.

The Divine Witness

7. God's Word is always right; choose to trust God's Word.

God always operates within the framework of his Word. The psalmist said, "Your word is a lamp to my feet and a light for my path" (Ps. 119:105). In most situations or concerns in life, we can find God's will revealed in the Bible. Even when the apostle Paul preached to the Bereans, they "examined the Scriptures every day to see if what Paul said was true" (Acts 17:11).

Bible reading, study, and meditation are critically important in our lives. The Bible is God's blueprint for living. The God who created us prepared this book so that we would understand him and know how to live our lives on earth. This book will constantly advise you and teach you God's ways. No other book is the divinely inspired Word of God, therefore we must make it part of our everyday lives.

Methodist founder John Wesley said:

> I am a creature of a day, passing through life as an arrow through the air. I am a spirit, coming from God, and returning to God; just hovering over the great gulf; a few months hence I am no more seen; I drop into an unchangeable eternity! I want to know one thing—the way to heaven. . . . God Himself has condescended to teach the way. He hath written it down in a book. O give me that Book! At any price, give me the book of God.[7]

And the great reformer Martin Luther years earlier had expressed a similar passion for the Word: "The Bible is alive, it speaks to me. It has feet, it runs after me. It has hands, it lays hold of me."[8]

Sometimes someone will say that he or she believes that this or that is God's will for someone else's life. Often when this happens the person's advice cannot be supported by Scripture. Thus, we must be cautious to turn to God's divine Word, for it is the foundation for all we do. When we spend time reading and studying the Bible, the Holy Spirit will help us in our daily decisions and make God's will known.

8. The Holy Spirit will lead you to truth; choose to trust the Holy Spirit's gentle leading.

Often we hear Christians say that they have a "check in their spirit" or "sense a red light." This is the way the Holy Spirit indicates that we should abstain from doing something or at least wait. When we witness in our spirits that something is not God's direction, we feel uncomfortable about a decision. God may be telling us to stop or slow down.

When we feel a check from God, it is not a vague bit of doubt; rather, it is similar to a chess game in which the king is exposed to an attack from which he must be protected or moved to safety. He is checked. The check involves stopping a forward course of action. We can see an example of this at the outset of Paul's second missionary journey. "When they came to the border of Mysia, they tried to enter Bithynia, but the Spirit of Jesus would not allow them to" (Acts 16:7). Very possibly the Lord stopped Paul from going to Bithynia by providing a situation in which he was prohibited from going where he had planned. As a result, Paul probably prayed about it and heard from the Lord that he should not go any further in that direction.

To make God's will operational in our lives, several things must line up: It must truly be God's will, the timing must be right, and the way his will is carried out must be just right. When any of these things is not present, we will be checked. We should not do something we feel uncomfortable about. This could be the Holy Spirit informing us to stop, slow down, or proceed at another time.

Over the years I have seen people miss God's will by moving too quickly. People often assume that God is directing them, so they move before the time is right. The more sensitized we become to the witness of the Spirit, the more we will recognize God's leading in the little things in our lives. Someone said, "Blessed is the man [or woman] who finds out which way God is moving and then gets going in the same direction."[9]

9. God will open and close doors; choose to look for God-orchestrated circumstances.

When God is orchestrating something we will not have to force the issue. God will intervene, and our lives will naturally flow in his will when we are yielded to him. Let me illustrate this. When I was a boy my family did jigsaw puzzles in our parsonage home on cold Minnesota winter nights. Periodically I would play a little game with my family. I would hold a piece of the puzzle because I knew that once the rest of the family got the jigsaw puzzle together, that last piece would drop into place, and I would get to complete the picture. Like a jigsaw puzzle, when God puts the pieces together, we don't have to force anything. The circumstances fit together.

Obedience Is Worth All Cost

IN THEIR BOOK *Making the Right Choices*, Ted Engstrom and Norman Rohrer tell this remarkable story:

> The scene is the Roman Empire just before Constantine when the persecution of Christians was outrageously commonplace.
>
> In the song, the decree goes out to Rome's military contingents that all soldiers be required to participate in a heathen ceremony praising the emperor. "Forty brave soldiers for Jesus," the song says, stood to reject the emperor's decree, announcing their allegiance instead to their Savior and Lord, Jesus Christ.
>
> Furious, the emperor had his troops build a bath house on a frozen lake to which the forty soldiers would be forced to march naked across the ice. When they arrived at the bath house, the emperor reasoned, all forty would gladly participate in the pagan sacrifice to their earthly ruler and save their skins.
>
> Only one soldier stood guard that night when the "forty brave soldiers for Jesus" took off all their clothing as commanded and started the march across the frozen lake to the bath house. The guard watched in awe as the Christians willingly walked barefoot and naked on the frozen water, singing songs of praise to the almighty God as they went. At the bath house, they lined up outside, still refusing to enter and participate in the ceremony.
>
> The eyes of the guard at the water's edge were riveted to the men as he marveled at their bravery and noted their resolve. Suddenly he saw one of them break ranks. The traitor turned to enter the bath house to recant his faith, and to obey Caesar. But the heat inside the bath house overcame the shivering body of the traitor and he died instantly.
>
> "Thirty-nine brave soldiers for Jesus" continued to sing songs to God and to worship the Creator as the soldier on

the shore watched with increasing awe. Suddenly he laid down his sword, took off his helmet, his uniform, and finally his boots and undergarments as well, then he started running across the ice. The thirty-nine soldiers cheered and embraced their brother in Christ and froze to death that night with the hymns of Zion on their lips.

"Forty brave soldiers for Jesus!" the story ends; nothing could change their true hearts. Only for truth would they stand there and die, only for life would they perish. That was a critical choice which they would have eternity to enjoy.[10]

The Choice Is Yours

THE TWENTIETH CENTURY WILL be recorded in the annals of history as a century of mind-boggling technological advancement, horrible world wars, vicious terrorism, rising and crumbling world powers, and among other things, a century in which the worldwide Christian church advanced in unprecedented ways. It will also be recorded that many world leaders were plagued with character crisis. Their agenda was to achieve power, prestige, promotion, or political or material gain at any cost. This attitude can become part of our lives too if we are not careful. If that occurs, there will be little in our lives to attract someone without Christ to the Christian life we claim to have.

George Barna's research indicates that people in the new millennium will choose whom they follow more carefully.

> No revolution can be victorious without strong, effective leaders. The cause of Christ in America is no different. While our trust must be placed in Him alone, He works through gifted leaders to mobilize, inspire, equip and direct us in the pursuit of His vision. But things are changing on the leadership front, too.
>
> In the past two decades Americans have been burned by leaders who oozed charisma and flashed world-class rhetorical skills but whose underlying character was debatable, at best. As expositors on leadership increasingly point to char-

acter as one of the core elements of great leaders, Americans will hone in on the inner stuff of those who wish to lead and will reject those whose character fails to meet the minimum acceptable standards.

Church leaders will undergo the same intense scrutiny as will our political, social, educational and business leaders. Pastors and lay leaders who possess valued functional skills will find their career paths blocked by their inability to demonstrate purity and depth of character. A double standard will be evident: the people in the pews, who do not meet up to the standards they set for their leaders, will increasingly withhold positions of leadership from skilled people who want to lead but also have glaring character flaws.[11]

In a similar way, unbelievers watch our lives with eyes of scrutiny. They watch to see if the Jesus we speak of really makes a difference in the way we live. They are looking for answers and listening for voices that are not just polished rhetorical homily but are presented by people who live Christlike lives, whose agendas are different from others, and whose kingdom is from another place.

Part Two

Embracing God's Vision

~⇒ FOUR ⇐~

The Beginning of the End

PEOPLE ALL AROUND THE country and the world have been intrigued with the tragic story of the *Titanic*. During much of 1997–98 when the Academy Award–winning film *Titanic* was being promoted, the Discovery Channel, documentary programs, CD-ROMs, and books were part of the media hype. Among other honors, the film received the award for "Best Picture" for its fascinating representation of the horrific event. The movie told of the "perfect" passenger ship, the largest, most luxurious ocean liner ever built, a ship that was considered unsinkable.[1]

Late in the night on April 14, 1912, during its maiden voyage, the huge ship scraped an iceberg, and its steel hull cracked. The deceptively giant chunk of ice (most of it under the surface of the water) punched holes through the *Titanic*'s side. Because of the tremendous pressure of the water rushing through the holes and crack, the hull broke open. Water rocketed in, and the beautiful ocean liner quickly fell to the bottom of the cold Atlantic.

People were dancing, sleeping, talking, and living in extravagance on board the ship during that last evening. Within seconds laughter turned to panic. Those who trusted the ingenuity of the manufacturers and the talent of those who operated the vessel were horror-struck when they became aware that they had little chance of surviving. People of tremendous wealth would have given all of it up for a chance to live. With little warning the ship took more than 1,500 people to their dark, watery graves and came to rest thousands of feet below the surface.

The pride that trusts human ingenuity as the source of greatness and perfection was evident as the *Titanic* was christened and
sent on its first and final cruise. The ship's sinking is a reminder of
the potential for arrogance among human beings.

You may remember that the twenty lifeboats that were
dropped over the side of the *Titanic* were only half full. The pas-
sengers in only one of these boats rowed back toward the screaming people who were trying to find something, anything, to cling
to. The others frantically rowed away, desperately trying to put as
much distance between themselves and the ship as they could.
They were relatively safe; the cries, the begging, and the pain of
those who would soon lose their lives had little effect on those who
were secure.

America, a Ship That Cannot Sink?

WE CAN DRAW A similar picture of the church in America. Most
Christians feel relatively safe and secure: they own homes and
automobiles, have jobs, worship in beautiful church buildings, and
can choose from numerous pastors in their community to listen
to on any given Sunday. Yet in this land of opportunity, our cities
are full of crime, our kids are using drugs, about half of our marriages are ending in divorce, our doctors are aborting over 1.5 million unborn children each year, suicide is becoming an epidemic
among teens and the elderly, and attendance at most churches is
standing still or declining. Nightly on world news reports we can
see gang violence, immorality among national leaders, militant
homosexuality, nations falling, terrorism, uncontrollable illnesses,
and famine that threatens the lives of millions. We as Christians
might be in the lifeboat, but people all around us are screaming
for help.

Much like the church in Laodicea, many in the church of
America say, "I am rich; I have acquired wealth and do not need
a thing" (Rev. 3:17). A paralyzing lethargy and complacency
plague this needy nation. Like Laodicea we have been deceived

into thinking we "have it all" and "do not need a thing." Could it be, however, that the Lord of the church would say, "I know your deeds, that you are neither cold nor hot.... You do not realize that you are wretched, pitiful, poor, blind and naked" (Rev. 3:15, 17)?

A Nation in Great Spiritual Need

AMERICA IS NOT A Christian nation. Only individuals are Christians. We are a nation that has been greatly blessed by God, but we must wake up to the fact that millions are turning their backs on God and sin is rapidly becoming rampant. The sins of our generation are at least as bad as those of the generations before us, and the temptations of today are more sophisticated, bold, deceptive and mind-boggling than ever before. Virtual reality might be able to help medical science, but it can also be used for sinful activities that would embarrass most of us. The Internet offers tremendous ability to communicate with libraries, colleges, professionals, retailers, and manufacturers. With this technology we can shop for almost anything from the privacy of our homes; however, some people are using the Internet to view some of the filthiest, most destructive pornography ever created.

On the *Family News in Focus* radio program, Bob McAllister commented:

> A decade ago, Gary Hart was forced to drop out of the Democratic presidential race when the media disclosed an extra-marital affair with Donna Rice. Hart had no choice. His popularity plummeted because voters did not want a man of questionable character running for the presidency.
>
> Ten years later, President Clinton enjoyed the highest approval ratings of his presidency despite mounting evidence that made Gary Hart look puritanical by comparison. In just a decade, public sentiment changed that much, suggesting that the secularization of society may be complete.
>
> Another indication of how far society came: 54 percent of Americans said Clinton was no worse than most men, which may be the single most telling statistic. Could it be

that this mess somehow confirms rampant lust in the hearts of average men and women and makes us feel better, less guilty? A host of lessors has filled that role before: Dennis Rodman, Ellen DeGeneres, Hugh Hefner—all exalted and glorified by a sex-saturated media intent on wiping out any lingering moral code.[2]

It is said that "a high percentage of the people of America attend church." That may be true; however, many who claim to attend church do it seldom or possibly just at Christmas or Easter. George Gallup says that weekly attendance at church, synagogue, or other places of worship is the lowest it has been since 1940 when only 37 percent of U.S. adults attended worship weekly. In 1996 only 38 percent reported weekly attendance, compared to a high of 49 percent in the late 1950s.[3] A significant number of churches today are dead. No gospel presentation that will set people free from the bondage of their sinful behavior is made in the services of these churches. If we do not quickly "realize" our condition, then I fear that the blessings we enjoy will be removed.

As Christians we must understand that we are in the lifeboat of the church of Jesus Christ; however, our job is not to row away from the screams of people, but to row toward them and pull as many as we can inside the boat.

H. B. London of Focus on the Family said:

> I read some disturbing facts recently that sobered me. Although Christianity is the largest religion in North America— 262 million by the year 2000—its overall rate of growth is exceeded by most of the other major religions. The .8% annual increase of Christianity is less than North America's growth rate of .9%. In other words, we are losing our "market share."
>
> By the year 2010, the number of Muslims in the U.S. will surpass the number of Jews, making it America's second largest faith. Most of our evangelical groups are growing at a rate of 1.5% of the total number of Christians in North America.
>
> What's the problem? From my perspective, we have lost our focus. We seem to be more interested in how we do

church than how we live, how we evangelize and what we believe. We are giving up too much substance for style.[4]

We can never get away from the fact that our personal life in Jesus Christ is the most significant critical factor in persuading people to want the God we serve.

You Can Make a Difference

MARK AND ALICE ARE missionaries in Colombia, South America. In a prayer letter to their supporting churches, they said:

> Driving through Christmas traffic, fighting the drizzling rain, I chanced on a 4-year-old girl. She was wet, cold and shaking. Her clothes were ragged; her hair was matted; her nose was running. She walked between the cars at the stop-light, washing headlights because she was too short to wash windshields. A few gave her coins; others honked at her to get away from their vehicles.
>
> As I drove away, only some 50 cents poorer, I raged at God for the injustice in the world that allowed the situation: "God, how could you just stand by, helpless?"
>
> Later that evening, God came to me softly with that small voice and responded not in like kind to my rage, but with tenderness, "I have done something. I created you."[5]

Mark and Alice are in Colombia as ambassadors for Christ. They can make a difference as they endeavor to reach the needy people of Colombia.

We are Christ's ambassadors in a very complicated land. This nation has received so much, we dare not keep it to ourselves. We might have tremendous wealth, power, and influence, but the sophisticated sin of our society is blinding millions from the reality of Jesus Christ.

Our young people are crying out for help today. If we attend a rock concert, we will hear screams of adoration toward musicians who promote disrespect and sex with people of the opposite sex, same sex, and even animals. We will hear verbiage that would offend almost anyone and see X-rated performances. We will see young people using illegal drugs and alcohol and engaging in sexual activities classified as indecent exposure. We will watch the crowd's bodies pulsate with the deafening sound of the band. After the concert is over, however, the mass of people will dissipate and the young people will be alone with their thoughts—and regrets.

David Wilkerson, founder of Teen Challenge, recently said:

> In our time, we've seen rock stars and music groups come and go. You may remember the eras of psychedelic rock, punk rock, and grunge rock. Now there is something called antichrist rock. Perhaps you've heard of the new band heralding this movement. They're called Marilyn Manson. They took their name from Marilyn Monroe and mass-murderer Charles Manson. And they're packing arenas and auditoriums around the country.
>
> Marilyn Manson is blatantly anti-Christ. One of their releases is titled "Antichrist Superstar," and the lyrics are blasphemous attacks on our Lord. As part of their stage act, they rip apart Bibles.
>
> I realize that such groups fade like grass. Even the Beatles—the group who once said they were more popular than Jesus—came and went. And I know Marilyn Manson will fade away as well. A few years from now, people who hear their name will ask, "Marilyn who?"
>
> Yet something is happening among young people in America right now—and I feel an urgency to address it. A few weeks ago, as Marilyn Manson was performing in Washington, D.C., one of their road crew fell from a wall and was killed. Yet, the group simply played on. They continued the concert in spite of the sudden death of their crew member.
>
> I bring this to your attention for a reason. I believe the antichrist lyrics of this group's music have become the language of our youth. Recently, I listened in horror as a group of teenagers and preteens discussed religion. Within minutes they had raised their voices and were shouting four-letter curses: "_____ God, _____ Jesus!"

As I looked into their faces, I saw an angry rebellion I'd never witnessed before. Blazing in their eyes was a hatred for religion. An antichrist attitude had completely overtaken them! Today young people no longer curse politicians, parents or society. They don't turn their anger against racism, poverty or discrimination. Nor is it enough for them simply to be antiestablishment. Now they have turned their fury against God and Christ![6]

I confess that I have at times looked at this type of behavior and for a few moments rejected the people. For many of our nation's young people, however, beneath all of their rebellion, reckless behavior, and cursing is a cry for help. "Would someone please tell me why I'm here and what life is all about?" Marilyn Manson was promoted as the final act of the MTV music awards for 1997. Curious about this popular rock group that tens of thousands of our children are enamored with, I decided to tune in and watch the segment. Marilyn Manson—the lead performer from whom the group takes its name—opened his "music" by coming to the podium and saying, "To free you from the fascism of Christianity. . . . Do you want to go to a place filled with [expletive deleted] holes?" This man's hatred for Christianity is as pronounced as any I have ever seen.

Wilkerson commented further, "I saw a newspaper photo of a group of Christian teens demonstrating outside an arena where Marilyn Manson was playing. This brave little band of believers was carrying signs protesting the group's blasphemous attacks against their Lord. I thank God such young people had chosen to stand up for Jesus."[7]

Some protests can be viewed as adversarial, but these young people were aware of the confusion that many of their friends were a part of, and they attempted to provide a "lifeboat" for the thousands who were letting their minds be influenced by one of the most hideous, satanic rock groups in the world. I pray that more of us would have this type of courage.

The Twentieth Century

THE TWENTIETH CENTURY SAW the greatest church growth world-wide of any century before it. Statisticians David Barrett and Todd Johnson predict that by the year 2000 the number of Christians on earth will exceed two billion for the first time in history. Christians today number 1.985 billion (using a fairly broad definition of "Christian"). At the present rate of growth, that number will reach 2.024 billion by the year 2000.[8] At the National Symposium on Postdenominational Church, missions statistician George Otis Jr. said:

> Out of all the people who have been saved since the time of Christ
>
> - 70% have been saved since 1900.
> - 70% of those have been saved since 1945.
> - 70% of those have been saved in the last 10 years.[9]

There is no question that Christianity could be at its greatest hour and could potentially fulfill the Great Commission of its Lord.

We wrote in *The Blessing: Experiencing the Power of the Holy Spirit Today,*

> I'm not sure that we can comprehend the numbers of people who are coming to Christ and all of the reasons why. Christianity is the fastest-growing religious movement in the world with a 6.9 percent growth rate per year. That compares to 2.7 percent for Islam, 2.2 percent for Hinduism, and 1.7 percent for Buddhism.
>
> Numerous denominations and parachurch groups are pulling out the stops in their efforts to increase world evangelism. It seems that, with the turn of the millennium, countless organizations have a new vision, and many are setting wonderful goals. Dick Eastman of Every Home for Christ, David Bryant of Concerts of Prayer International, and many others are committed to enlisting and mobilizing the largest prayer movement in the history of the church. They, and we,

are convinced that every revival has begun with prayer. Furthermore, the most creative means and effective technological equipment the church has ever used are now available. More than 2,500 Christian radio and television stations daily broadcast the gospel of Jesus Christ to a potential 4.6 billion of the world's population.... In the next few years, we will see a tremendous increase of propagating the gospel of Jesus Christ by satellite communication and the Internet.

Speaking of evangelism in our day, Neil Anderson writes:

Not since the Day of Pentecost have we seen such a phenomenal growth of the church worldwide. For example, Africa was less than five percent Christian at the turn of the century; Africa is expected to be 50 percent Christian by the end of this millennium. In 1950 China had only one million believers; now it is estimated that one hundred million are coming to Christ annually. Indonesia is the world's most populated Muslim nation, but the percentage of Christians has been progressing so rapidly that the government won't release accurate figures. In 1900 South Korea did not have a single evangelical church; in 1992 South Korea had 37,500 churches. Globally, the Holy Spirit has woven together a massive cooperative effort that could produce a harvest of at least one billion souls in the next five years. The church could be experiencing the first fruits of the greatest awakening it has ever known.[10]

The Terminal Generation

WE COULD BE THE terminal generation who will experience the rapture of the church. The Bible tells us that "this gospel of the kingdom will be preached in the whole world as a testimony to all nations, and then the end will come" (Matt. 24:14).

Never in the history of the world has "this gospel" had such widespread exposure to all of the nations like it has today. Through radio, satellite, the Internet, the printed page, and an army of missionaries from every denomination, the gospel is constantly being propagated. This is the greatest opportunity the church has ever had, and we are seeing more people worldwide come to know Jesus Christ as Lord and Savior than at any other time in the history of the church. If we put all these factors in place—more open doors than at any other time, more technology, more missionaries, more denominations and parachurch groups joining together to share the gospel with everyone in the world—we could be at the very hour when we could see the words of Paul fulfilled: "For the Lord himself will come down from heaven, with a loud command, with the voice of the archangel and with the trumpet call of God, and the dead in Christ will rise first. After that, we who are still alive and are left will be caught up together with them in the clouds to meet the Lord in the air" (1 Thess. 4:16–17).

It is sad that we denominations have let doctrinal differences separate us in the past. But I see a new day when many will share a common goal to ensure that every man, woman, and child hears the gospel of Jesus Christ.

One such organization has joined together with every evangelical denomination and parachurch group with the goal of praying for and exposing every family in America to the gospel by the end of the year 2000. It is as if many are driven to finish the task and get the job done. We are in sight of the goal and could very well be the people who are alive when Jesus' commission has been completed.

The Task Before Us

THE REASON JESUS CHRIST came to the world two thousand years ago was to "seek and to save what was lost" (Luke 19:10). The will of God for every Christian today is to do the same in the power of the Holy Spirit. Jesus commanded us to "Go into all the world and preach the good news to all creation" (Mark 16:15). The colleagues that work alongside you, the men or women with whom you take a coffee break, your unsaved family members, and those who live around you are important to God. Are you concerned about their eternal destiny? Do you care where they spend eternity? Have you prayed and asked God to show you ways to present the gospel of Jesus Christ to them? Or are you consumed with trying to survive and provide for your family and protect what you own?

Jesus informed a small band of disciples that it was their task to take the gospel to the entire world. These people were just as ordinary as you and me. They had little, if any, charismatic talent or reputation. They were insignificant, uneducated men and women who didn't have great wealth or technological advantage. There is no question that Jesus believed in them; he knew what he was doing, and he was confident that they could do everything he asked them to do. In fact, he was laying the future of his church on their shoulders.

When Jesus gave these new believers the challenge, Rome ruled the world. They were to go to Rome and inform Caesar and his followers that there is only one "Lord," and that Lord is Jesus Christ, the Creator of all things. They were to go to pagan Greece and inform the people of Athens that Jesus is the only way to heaven. They were to inform people of all religions, philosophies, and superstitions that they could have a personal relationship with the living God through his Son Jesus Christ. And they were to tell those caught up in trying to work their way to heaven that God had made provision for them through the cross and the resurrection of Jesus.

The Lord's command was to go to every nation on the earth, learn the languages and live with the people, pray for the sick, command demons to leave those who were possessed, and explain the gospel to everyone they could. They were to walk into places where demons had taken control and boldly proclaim that Jesus Christ broke the back of Satan's power when he rose from the dead.

The early disciples were as fearful as you or me. Very probably they said, "How in the world can we do this? It's impossible. There is no way it can be done. Does he realize who he is talking to? I am weak. I don't have a lot of talent, and my communication skills simply aren't there!" They may have wondered, "How can we take the gospel to a world that hated Jesus so much that they killed him? How can we go into other parts of the world when we have no money? What will make people listen to us? How can I learn another language when I have so little education?"

Jesus had the answers for all of their questions then, and today he has the answers to all of our questions. Be assured of this: God will always enable us to do everything he asks us to do. Paul said, "I can do everything through him who gives me strength" (Phil. 4:13). The early church didn't have the massive personal or technological advancements that we have, which means that they weren't slaves to these advancements either. They didn't have ungodly television programs that promote sin and mock righteousness. They didn't have multimillion-dollar movies and videos that fascinate viewers with shameful behaviors and verbiage. They didn't have computer sex, virtual reality sex, or porno magazines. The devil has done everything he can to paralyze and neutralize the church through these hideous mediums.

Satan could not stop the disciples of the first century from what some might call a revolutionary movement, and he cannot stop today's disciples. The message is the same, the power is still available, and we have more numbers and more helps than ever before.

Jesus knew what our generation would face. He knew exactly what the last days would be about. He knew that Satan would endeavor to deceive the very elect—us. Because Jesus understands and knows all things, he foresaw the moral condition of our generation. Human behavior continues to become depraved, and the hateful devil continues to persecute and attack the church in horrible ways.

The disciples to whom Jesus was speaking wondered how they would have the strength to do what he commanded. At times I also have wondered how I can do what God has asked me to do. Perhaps you have asked the same question. The gift Jesus gave the early church is ours too. He said, "I am going to send you what my Father has promised; but stay in the city until you have been clothed with power from on high" (Luke 24:49). After Jesus' resurrection he reminded them of this promise again; "But you will receive power when the Holy Spirit comes on you; and you will be my witnesses in Jerusalem, and in all Judea and Samaria, and to the ends of the earth" (Acts 1:8).

God understands the obstacles and the resistance we will face. He knows about the rejection, sneers, and even the persecution that some of us will go through. But he has provided for us a power greater than any other force in the universe with which we can stand against governments, leaders, kings, demons, and principalities. We cannot get this power through education, talent, or heredity. It comes only from God. We need only ask God for it and hold steady until he gives it to us.

Jesus never would have asked us to reach this world with the gospel unless he knew we would have the power to do it. The disciples had weaknesses just like we do. They had fears, insecurities, and feelings of inadequacy. In fact, they ran when their leader was taken from them. They were fearful about taking a stand for their Lord. Instead of "going for it," they went fishing. They were timid and unskilled, yet Jesus knew that if they fully submitted to the Holy Spirit, God would perform miracles through them and they would be able to send demons running everywhere they went.

When the Holy Spirit filled the disciples, they were never the same. They fearlessly began witnessing for their Lord as never before. A boldness that was beyond human courage consumed their lives. The Holy Spirit gave them words that cut through human rhetoric. They spoke with authority, wisdom, and might because they had received the power Jesus had promised them.

The crowds that had mocked the disciples' Lord only weeks before were now afraid of them. Literally thousands decided to become Christians when Peter preached his first sermon after he received the gift of the baptism in the Holy Spirit. The disciples went to villages, towns, temples, and homes preaching and explaining the life-changing message of Jesus Christ. These timid, uneducated, fearful men were never the same.

Jesus offers this same power to us. There has been an incredible advance of the gospel in the twentieth century, but billions of people are yet unreached. Multitudes of people who call themselves Christians but are not born again need to be reached, and churches that were once alive and vibrant need to be stirred again. The same Holy Spirit who anointed, empowered, and gave strategy to the early church will give the same to the church in the twenty-first century.

Jaci Velasquez is a nineteen-year-old recording artist whose album *Heavenly Places* is one of the highest-selling debut efforts in Christian music. She was nominated for four Dove Awards, and her songs have communicated the gospel to multitudes of young people. When Jaci was twelve years old, her family decided that God had called them to a career in ministry. The committed family put their household goods in storage, climbed into their motor home, and began a musical ministry by faith. God always provided for the family. Jaci's talent in singing developed, and today she says the high point of her life is her ability to reach more people for Jesus Christ. Jaci's advice to young people wherever she goes is, "Be a servant where God has you and serve Him with your whole heart."[11]

Your circle of influence might not be like Jaci's through incredible musical talent. It may not be the ability to reach Europe, Cuba, or even your own state. For many of us, our influence extends to our family, our neighbors, and the people with whom we work. The expectations for us are just the same as for a person like Billy Graham, James Dobson, or David Cho (who pastors the largest church in the world). We must reach those around us with the gospel of Jesus Christ. We need to pray that the Holy Spirit will convict and open the hearts of the people to whom we are supposed to witness.

In his weekly newsletter to pastors, H. B. London of Focus on the Family said:

> This week I took note of the *USA Today* Snapshots on our "Growing World." It predicted a worldwide population of 6 billion people by the end of the year. It also mentioned that there were 136,967,149 births each year and 53,282,252 deaths—but to make it even more sobering, there are 15,636

births each hour and 6,082 deaths, or 261 people born each minute and 101 that die. That's every 60 seconds!

We estimate that approximately 39% of the adult population in the USA are born again. I wonder how many in North America die without the saving knowledge of Jesus Christ?

I can remember a day when personal witnessing and an urgency for the lost was on the front burner of nearly every church in America.[12]

Though programs in our churches are critically important for the discipling of believers, most people will not find Christ through these various programs. By far, the majority of people come to Christ because we as individuals share the Good News with our family, friends, and workmates.

As I travel around the world, I notice a sense of anticipation among Christians. Believers from every denomination sense that we could be getting close to that day when the Lord promised he would take the church from this world. Only God knows when the task will be finished. He is patient, not wanting anyone to perish; nevertheless, there will be a day when he says to his Son, "The job is finished; the church has done what we have asked it to do."

Perhaps you have heard the story of the lighthouse that stood atop a dangerous cliff warning sailors of the jagged rocks below. Those who lived in the lighthouse often went out in small boats to rescue people from sinking ships. Over the years they remodeled the lighthouse to make it more comfortable by adding lounge chairs, a big-screen TV, air conditioning, and a pool table. All this new stuff was expensive, so they began spending most of their time raising funds.

The lighthouse became more like a club than a rescue station. So people in a nearby town formed a rescue society to save drowning people. The lighthouse group had forgotten their original purpose.[13]

As we face the challenge of a new millennium, many wonder if the church in America will lose its cutting edge—perhaps one of the greatest reasons why God raised up this blessed nation. Someone said:

If we could shrink the earth's population to a village of precisely 100 people, with all existing human ratios remaining the same, it would consist of the following:

- There would be 57 Asians, 21 Europeans, 14 from the Western Hemisphere (both North and South, of which 6 would be American), and 8 Africans.
- 70 would be nonwhite, 30 white.
- 70 would be non-Christian, 30 Christian.
- Half of the world's entire wealth would be in the hands of only six people. All six would be Americans.
- 70 would be illiterate, 30 literate.
- 50 would be malnourished; 50 would be adequately fed.
- 80 would live in substandard housing; 20 would be adequately housed.
- Only one would have a college education.[14]

Are we, the church in America, ready for fresh vision, renewed commitment, and a new energy that only the Holy Spirit can give, or will we decline and lose the drive that we once had to evangelize all of the lost?

On December 31, A.D. 1000, masses of people met outside the walls of the Vatican waiting for the end of the world. Just like any other night, it came and went. The pope encouraged everyone to go home. History records that the church was virtually at a standstill for approximately the next five hundred years. People didn't see a lost and dying world. Many didn't hear the cries of the multitudes who were looking for answers. The church became self-centered and passive, and it lost its original vision.

Now, a thousand years later, billions of people are waiting, wondering what will happen in the new millennium. The challenge remains the same; the need has never been greater; the devil has never worked harder. The difference is that we are closer than ever before to the rapture of the church, and we are within sight of reaching every people group with the glorious gospel of Jesus Christ. We must not "become weary in doing good."

The Look of Love

KARLA WAS A DAUGHTER of a prostitute. She began using dope at eight and became a heroin addict at age twelve. Like her mother, she turned to prostitution at age fourteen, and her already hardened heart became tougher as she experienced men who used her young body to fulfill their sick lusts. From the start of her life, it seemed she didn't stand a chance—she was on a downward spiral toward destruction. It seemed that nothing could stop her reckless lifestyle of hate, rebellion, and lawlessness. As foolhardy as her behavior was, few could imagine her degree of unrestraint. Her hotheaded, uncaring actions, would eventually end her life.

According to prison records, in June of 1983, twenty-three-year-old Karla Faye Tucker and her boyfriend, Daniel Ryan Garrett, were both high on an array of drugs from a three-day binge. They sneaked into Jerry Lynn Dean's apartment to steal motorcycle parts. In what became a grizzly confrontation, Garrett used a hammer and Tucker used a pickax to kill Dean. When Deborah Thornton was found hiding beneath a blanket in Dean's room, Tucker rushed her and viciously swung the pickax into Deborah's body over and over again. Police reports state that both victims had more than twenty stab or puncture wounds, and the pickax was found imbedded in Thornton's chest.

This inhuman act caused many to think that Karla Faye was without a conscience, that she was a sociopath. If she felt remorse for the murders, few, if any, knew about it. Her heart was cold and fixed on doing whatever her care-free, drug-altered mind told her to do.

On February 3, 1998, Karla was executed by lethal injection in perhaps one of the most highly publicized executions in the history of the United States—highly publicized because she was the first woman since the middle of the Civil War to be put to death in the state of Texas. Also, up to the moment of her death, she expressed her remorse to the Thornton and Dean families and spoke of the changes Jesus Christ had made in her life. What happened to the tough, hateful Karla?

Not long after Karla was incarcerated, fifteen years before her death, Johnathan and Karen Gill had brought a puppet show to the Harris County Jail.

Karla Faye recalled, "All the women in my unit were going to this puppet show in the chapel. I didn't want to go, but I didn't want to be alone either, so I thought I would go and just socialize with the other women. The second I walked through the door, I felt something. I know now that it was the presence of God."

Karen Gill had also spent time in jail, and through a ministry program called Teen Challenge in Houston, both she and Johnathan were helped and in turn became involved in ministry to those in jail or prison. Through the puppet show Karen communicated the love of God and the forgiveness she had found in Jesus Christ.

Karla Faye said, "These people were where I had been. There was a glow about them—a peace that was so real. I wanted to have what they had. I wanted to feel what they felt."

The evening of the puppet show, Karla Faye didn't speak to anyone. She watched, she listened, and for some reason she heard what the little puppets were saying. Strangely, toughness started to melt; she felt feelings she had never felt before, and she secretly took one of the free Bibles to her cell. She sat in the corner of her cell and started to read God's Word.

"I couldn't understand what I was reading," Karla said, "but the next thing I knew, I was in the middle of the floor on my knees

crying out for God to forgive me. At that time, I don't know if I felt
forgiven, but I felt his love surround me . . . like a cocoon."

Her mind began thinking thoughts she had previously refused
to accept. She felt that God was enabling her to face the heartless
murders she had committed. In waves of emotion, she began to
sob as the full impact of her crimes came over her. Even though
she now understood her horrible actions and the helplessness of
her life, she sensed God's presence in that jail cell.

She said, "The whole time, God was loving me."

The message of the puppet ministry eternally impacted Karla.
She unconditionally surrendered her life to Christ and for fifteen
years she grew in the Christian faith.

Some might say, "That's convenient; she decided to pick up
jailhouse religion in order to gain clemency. She was so corrupt
that she would even use God to save herself from the execution
chamber."

Those who knew Karla only speak of a changed person.

Chaplain Alexander Taylor, a regional program administrator
for the Texas Department of Criminal Justice, said, "She was a
powerful witness for God for many years—it's difficult being a
Christian in prison. If you're a fake, you'll be found out quickly."

Chaplain Jerry Groom, administrator of chaplaincy programs
for the Texas Department of Criminal Justice said, "Karla's life
expressed a tremendous sense of having received God's forgiveness and acceptance. She was repentant, dedicated to giving back
to those from whom she had taken."

"Her life has forever impacted my life and inspires me to this
day," Groom added. "Having walked to heaven's gate with Karla,
I was left with a fresh appreciation for God's grace and power to
transform."

Jim Brazzil, the chaplain who stayed with Karla Faye in the
execution chamber, said, "In the midst of all the hardship and all
the trials, she was the one encouraging everyone."

The day before Karla's execution, knowing that Jim would
speak at her funeral, Karla wrote an encouraging note to him and

put it in his Bible. Jim said, "It really blessed me and ministered to me in a way that I really needed at that time."

Karla Faye's last statement was:

> I would like to say to all of you, the Thornton family and Jerry Dean's family, that I am so sorry. I hope God will give you peace with this.
> Baby, I love you. [to her husband]
> Ron [friend and brother of Deborah Thornton], give Peggy [friend and sister of Jerry Dean] a hug for me. Everybody has been so good to me.
> I love all of you very much. I am going to be face-to-face with Jesus now.
> Warden Baggett [Mountain View warden], thank all of you so much. You have been so good to me. I love all of you very much. I will see you all when you get there. I will wait for you.[1]

How Big Is God's Love?

DO YOU BELIEVE THAT God loves everyone? Do you believe that God can change anyone, no matter what he or she has done? How about someone who has lived a homosexual life or who is a drug pusher, a dishonest politician, a rapist, or a child molester? Even closer to home, how about someone who has done a terrible thing to you? Do you believe God loves that person? Until you grasp the magnitude of God's love for you and for others, you will have a difficult time believing that God wants to reach everyone regardless of his or her sinful condition. The Bible tells us, "God so loved the world that he gave his one and only Son, that whoever believes in him shall not perish but have eternal life" (John 3:16). God's love embraces everyone in the world regardless of lifestyle, nationality, age, or color.

By giving his Son as an offering for sin, God provided atonement for *everyone*. Humans are reconciled back to God because of the life and death of Jesus Christ. Jesus bore our sins in his own body on the cross, "the righteous for the unrighteous, to bring [us] to God" (1 Peter 3:18). As human beings, it is difficult to comprehend exactly what happened when Christ died on the cross, forever changing the heart of God toward sinful humanity. By offering himself, Christ provided perfect and complete redemption for the sins of the world. God's love for us motivated him to give his absolute best. This is the grace of God. We didn't deserve it and we can't earn it—God simply moved in and did for us what we could not do for ourselves.

The physical resurrection of Jesus Christ and his subsequent ascension into heaven bring the cross to the center of our eternal future. Some may ask, "What was the purpose of Christ dying if he had the power to rise from the dead?" The Bible tells us, "He was delivered over to death for our sins and was raised to life for our justification" (Rom. 4:25). Not only did Jesus provide a way for us to be forgiven and justified, but he took away the Enemy's power over death; "having disarmed the powers and authorities, he made a public spectacle of them, triumphing over them by the cross" (Col. 2:15).

Karla Faye was offered "redemption," and she humbly accepted the gift of salvation. Jesus Christ paid the price and took the punishment for her sins when he suffered and died on the cross (Isa. 53:10).

Paul said to the Corinthian church, "Do you not know that the wicked will not inherit the kingdom of God? Do not be deceived: Neither the sexually immoral nor idolaters nor adulterers nor male prostitutes nor homosexual offenders nor thieves nor the greedy nor drunkards nor slanderers nor swindlers will inherit the kingdom of God. And *that is what some of you were*. But you were washed, you were sanctified, you were justified in the name of the Lord Jesus Christ and by the Spirit of our God" (1 Cor. 6:9–11, italics added). The Corinthian church was full of ex-prostitutes, ex-adulterers, ex-thieves, ex-gays, and ex-sexual addicts. It is a picture of the church today. If you ask enough Christian people—and if they are transparent with you—you will discover Christian people who have been delivered from every kind of destructive behavior known to humankind. The love of God reaches out to all.

The Drawing Power of God's Love

IN 1867 THE GREAT EVANGELIST D. L. Moody visited Ireland and met a young teacher-preacher by the name of Harry Moorehouse. Moorehouse was a small, clean-shaven, boyish man with a heavy Lancashire accent. He was a converted pickpocket.

"If I am ever in Chicago, I'll preach for you," offered Moorehouse.

"If you come west, call on me," offered Moody, perhaps not really expecting to hear from him again.

But Moorehouse did come, and Moody did let him preach. Night after night, Harry Moorehouse preached on John 3:16.

At first Moody was openly annoyed at Moorehouse's selection of such a familiar Bible text and this night-after-night exposition of the same theme. He would begin with the text and then illustrate the love of God from other Scripture accounts. His message was different every night, but the theme and the text were always the same.

Something beautiful and life-changing began to happen to Moody. The truth of God's love began to overwhelm his soul! He saw God from a new perspective. Before, all he had seen was the wrath of God and his hatred for sin. Now he saw, as he had never seen before, the depth of God's compassion and his love and mercy to sinners. D. L. Moody was never the same again.

Moody said, "I never knew up to that time that God loved me so much. This heart of mine began to thaw out; I just couldn't keep back the tears. I just drank it all in. I will tell you, there is one thing that draws above everything else, and that is the love of God." He commented later, "I took up that word love and I do not know how many weeks I spent in studying the passages in which it occurs, till at last I could not help loving people! I had been feeding on love so long that I was anxious to do good to everybody I came in contact with."[2]

Think about Moody's experience. He was already a committed Christian. In fact, he was a powerful preacher who had traveled far away from home to communicate the gospel. Yet even he did not understand God's far-reaching love. Many of us are no different than D. L. Moody. We are believers, yet we do not understand how much God loves us and how much he loves the people around us. This lack of understanding may be due to a number of things: a significant person's rejection of us, an experience of being wounded by someone we trusted, or maybe just never choosing to think about the vastness of God's love for us. Understanding God's love will be a tremendous help to us and will encourage us to reach out to those around us. Sadly, because most of us have been hurt by someone, many choose to be angry with or even hateful to a person whom God is desperately trying to reach with his love.

What Does God's Love Look Like?

We Cannot Comprehend God's Love

David said:

When I consider your heavens,
    the work of your fingers,
the moon and the stars,
    which you have set in place,
what is man that you are mindful of him,
    the son of man that you care for him? (Ps. 8:3–4)

I've asked God the same question. On a clear night I sometimes look at the stars and say, "God, you have created all of those stars; all of them have been named by you—not any of them is missing [see Isa. 40:25–26], yet because of your love, you have your eye on me and you care for me. Why?" One of the reasons I have asked this question is that I know me. I understand that without Christ I am hopeless—and so are you.

The Bible informs us that there are no righteous people (Rom. 3:10); our ways are not God's ways (Isa. 53:6); our thoughts are not God's thoughts; our eyes do not see as God sees; our ears do not hear as God hears; our minds are twisted and constantly want to do things our way. Everyone has sinned (Rom. 3:23), and without Christ we cannot live a righteous life. Everyone—including Karla Faye Tucker, Harry Moorehouse, D. L. Moody, Thomas E. Trask, Wayde I. Goodall, and you—is a hopeless sinner without Christ. Our sin is sickening to God because he is absolutely pure, holy, and righteous. Any of us can love someone who does good things and acts in ways that make us happy, but how about loving people whose behavior offends or disgusts you? God hates sin. Our sin offends the Father and grieves the Holy Spirit, "but God demonstrates his own love for us in this: While we were still sinners, Christ died for us" (Rom. 5:8).

On countless occasions I have talked to people who feel horrible about their lives. They are overwhelmed with guilt and think there is no way God can forgive them and love them. Without hesitation, I encourage them to turn to the God who will always love them, who is always there, ready to forgive, forget, and welcome them into his family.

Years ago two young couples from the Philadelphia Church in Stockholm, Sweden, answered God's call to be missionaries to the Belgian Congo in Africa.

When David and Svea Flood and Joel and Bertha Erikson arrived at the mission station in 1921, they literally hacked their way with machetes into the interior. They finally reached a village, but the people said, "We can't allow any white people here, or our gods will be offended." At the next village, they were also rejected. The weary families had no choice. They settled in the jungle and built mud huts.

Soon they were plagued with loneliness, malnutrition, and sickness. After about six months, the Eriksons decided to return to the mission station. But Svea couldn't travel because she was pregnant with her second child and had malaria.

For several months Svea endured a raging fever. During that time, she witnessed to a little boy who came from a nearby village to sell chickens. He also brought fruit for the family. As Svea spoke to him, he simply smiled. She didn't know if he understood the message of Jesus Christ that she tried to communicate to him.

Svea delivered a healthy baby girl on April 13, 1923, but within a week Svea was at the point of death. In her final moments, she whispered to her husband, "Name our new baby Aina." Svea died seventeen days after Aina's birth.

David made a casket, and in a grave on the mountainside he buried his beloved wife. As he stood beside her grave, he looked down at his two-year-old son, David Jr. Then he heard his baby daughter's cries from the mud hut. Bitterness began to fill his heart. He flew into a rage, crying, "Why did you allow this, God? My wife was so beautiful, so talented, a soloist in the Philadelphia Church in Stockholm; now she lies dead at twenty-seven.

"I have a two-year-old son I can hardly care for, let alone a baby girl. After more than a year in this jungle, all we have to show for it is one little village boy who probably doesn't understand what Svea told him."

David Flood hired some tribesmen as guides and took his children to the mission station. When he saw the Eriksons, he blurted out angrily, "I'm leaving. I'm taking my son with me back to Sweden, but I'm leaving my daughter here with you."

When David arrived in Stockholm, he went into the import business. He warned those around him never to mention God in his presence. Eventually he began drinking heavily.

Shortly after David and his son left, and within three days of each other, the Ericksons died. Some suspected poisoning. Little Aina was given to an American Assemblies of God missionary couple—Arthur and Anna Berg. The Bergs took Aina to a village called Massisi in northern Congo. They named her Agnes and called her Aggie.

Alone much of the time, Aggie played games of imagination. She imagined she had brothers and a sister and even gave them names. She played with the African children and spoke Swahili.

When the Bergs returned to the United States, they brought Aggie. She had been born in the Congo of Swedish parents and had only a birth certificate with no evidence of Swedish citizenship and no Congolese citizenship. She was given a six-month alien visa to enter America, and for many years the Bergs had to travel to Canada to renew Aggie's visa and then reenter the United States. Aggie was a girl without a country. Many years later, after Aggie was married to an American and had her own family, she was able to become a U.S. citizen.

Over and over Aggie tried to put the pieces of her life together. Where was her father? What was he doing? Where was her brother David, and did she have other brothers and sisters? Forty years later she finally traveled to Stockholm to try to locate her father. Three half brothers greeted her at the hotel. She quickly asked them, "Where is David?" They pointed across the lobby to a man slumped in a chair. Like his father, he had nearly destroyed his life with alcohol.

When Aggie asked about her father, her brothers flushed with anger. None of them had talked to him in years.

Aggie's half sister arrived at the hotel. "All my life I've dreamed about you," she said. "I used to spread out a map of the world, put a toy car on it, and pretend to drive everywhere to find you."

Aggie and her sister went to find their father. They drove to an impoverished area of Stockholm, where they entered a rundown building and climbed the stairs to the third floor. Inside, liquor bottles lay everywhere. Lying on a bed in the corner was her father—the one-time missionary, David Flood. He was now seventy-three and suffering from diabetes. He had also had a stroke. Cataracts covered both of his eyes. Aggie fell to his side, crying, "Daddy, I'm your little girl—the one you left behind in Africa."

Tears formed in his eyes. "I never meant to give you away. I just couldn't handle both you and your brother."

Aggie answered, "That's okay, Daddy. God took care of me."

Her father's face became tight. "God didn't take care of you. He ruined our whole family. He led us to Africa and then betrayed us. Nothing ever came of our time there. It was a waste."

A short time before her visit, Aggie had received a Swedish magazine article in the mail that told the story of her mother, Svea Flood, and how many African churches revered her memory. It showed a picture of Svea's grave and told how her life and death had influenced the spread of the gospel in Zaire. Aggie told her father the story so that he could see that her mother had not died in vain.

Then Aggie sang hymns, as her mother had done, and prayed with him. He broke. Tears of sorrow and repentance flowed down his face, and he recommitted his life to Christ.

Not long after that meeting, David Flood died. Later Aggie learned that in his final days her father had begun painting scenes of Africa. In his final hours, delirious, he had begun speaking in Swahili. Before God took him home, he took him back to Africa.

When visiting London a few years later, Aggie and her husband were introduced to the Superintendent of the Pentecostal church in Zaire (the former Congo). His name was Ruhigita Ndagora. With curiosity, Aggie asked, "Did you ever know the missionaries David and Svea Flood?"

"Yes," he answered, "Svea Flood led me to Jesus Christ when I was just a boy. They had a baby girl, but I don't know what happened to her."

Aggie cried out, "I'm that girl! I'm Aina."

Ruhigita was the African boy who sold chickens and brought the Floods fruit. He was the only person in the Congo Svea Flood had led to Christ. From that one boy thousands of others were reached for Christ, and Ruhigita became a dynamic leader for the gospel in Zaire.[3]

The love of God is beyond comprehension. God cared about a little boy who sold chickens. God's love never gave up on David Flood, though he became bitter and ran from God much of his life. God's love would not let one of his children (Svea) die in vain; through her death thousands came to Christ. God's love kept Aggie, and the Holy Spirit led her all of her life.

God's love can be difficult to understand, because we live in a world where people limit their love. Couples make vows to love and to cherish each other for a lifetime, but one or both often break their vows. Parents give up on children; children give up on parents. People refuse to forgive or to ask for forgiveness. The media constantly inundates our homes with a message that says love has its limits and that when the emotion is gone, love is gone. God's love has no limits. It reaches out to everyone all the time. His love is not predicated on whether we choose to accept or reject it. It is his very nature to love, because "God is love" (1 John 4:16).

God's Love Is Without Measure

God gave his best, his only Son. I can't imagine giving one of my sons for someone else, even though I have three. Such love is beyond human reasoning, yet there is no other way for God to reconcile us to himself.

Jesus Christ was sinless and had no guilt. Like you and me, he was tempted in all ways; but unlike us, he did not yield to his temptations. The writer of Hebrews tells us, "We do not have a high priest who is unable to sympathize with our weaknesses, but we have one who has been tempted in every way, just as we are—yet was without sin" (4:15). Jesus did not deserve to die. "He committed no sin, and no deceit was found in his mouth" (1 Peter 2:22).

A sinless sacrifice was necessary to provide forgiveness and cleansing for our sins. Paul wrote, "God made him who had no sin to be sin for us, so that in him we might become the righteousness of God" (2 Cor. 5:21). When we make Jesus Christ our Lord and ask him for forgiveness for our sins, he completely forgives us of every sin we have committed and cleanses us from that sin (see 1 John 1:9). We are then "born again" (John 3:3) and "become the righteousness of God." Our righteousness is because of what Jesus did for us on the cross. When Jesus was nailed to the cross, he bore our sin and paid the price for it. During those hours when Jesus hung there, he cried out to his Father, *"Eloi, Eloi, lama sabachthani*?" which means, "My God, my God, why have you for-saken me?" (Matt. 27:46). Because God is a pure and holy God, he could not even look at his sinless Son who had taken our sins upon himself on the cross. Jesus took the curse and the punishment for us (see Gal. 3:13).

Think of the most embarrassing, evil, mean, or selfish sin you have committed. All of us can think of something we have done or said that we would love to take back. But it's done—we can't take the words or activity back. However, with our sincere repentance, God will completely forgive us and forget it.

Do you understand that you can't measure God's love? There has never been any love like it since the creation of the world. If you are trying to comprehend how much God loves you, look at the cross. "This is how we know what love is: Jesus Christ laid down his life for us" (1 John 3:16). Your sins, my sins, and the sins of everyone were paid for because of God's love.

Before we become Christians, we live in "the dominion of darkness," but after we give our lives to Christ, we can be assured that we have been rescued from that satanic dominion and have been brought into the "kingdom of the Son [God] loves" (see Col. 1:13). Paul tells us that because Jesus suffered on the cross, "God made you alive with Christ. He forgave us all our sins" (Col. 2:13). The way to appropriate Christ's provision for our lives is to make him the Lord of our lives by repenting of our sins and choosing to obey him.

What have you done that you are ashamed of? Who have you hurt? How stuck are you in a terrible habit, or how mean and angry do you feel? There are no big or little sins. All sins need to be forgiven and will be—the *moment* you ask.

While we must know that God absolutely loves us, we must also understand that he is not lax when dealing with sin. God hates the sin but loves the person. Sin ruins the people he loves; therefore, when we become involved in any sin, he understands what it can potentially do to us. He never ignores sin but demands that we repent and be obedient to him. This is something every one of us must *choose* to do. We choose to make Jesus Christ our Lord. We choose to ask for forgiveness. We choose to live a life that is pleasing to him. We choose how close to Jesus we will walk. And we choose to demonstrate God's love by the way we treat people.

What Does a Christian's Love Look Like?

THE BIBLE TELLS US that "whoever does not love does not know God, because God is love" (1 John 4:8). Erwin Lutzer said, "One cannot love his neighbor unless he loves God."[4] He also said, "God loved the world. Go thou and do likewise."[5]

We feel differently about people and treat them differently when we have a relationship with Jesus Christ. We are kinder and more forgiving and merciful, and we reflect the love of God. I like what Augustine said: "What does love look like? It has hands to help others. It has feet to hasten to the poor and needy. It has eyes to see misery and want. It has ears to hear the sighs and sorrows of men. That is what love looks like."[6] And in our day Max Lucado has said, "Plant a word of love heart-deep in a person's life. Nurture it with a smile and a prayer, and watch what happens."[7] This kind of love attracts people to our faith.

Church growth expert Charles Arn wrote in his book *Who Cares About Love?* that non-Christians are attracted to God's love when they experience the love of God's people. Through intensive research he discovered the following:

- Loving churches are growing churches. Churches that demonstrate love in a variety of ways (to their members and nonmembers in the community) are growing. Churches that demonstrate less love have less growth.
- Visitors are more loved in growing churches. On a scale of 1 to 10, how loving do you feel your church is to visitors?
- Growing churches express greater love to their community. They find ways to help the people of their community—their neighbor.

- The amount of love a church expresses is unrelated to the size of its surrounding community. Whether rural, suburban, or downtown churches—it makes no difference. Churches that demonstrate love in concrete ways grow more.
- Members of growing churches experienced love to a greater degree than members of plateaued or declining churches regardless of church size.[8]

In response to this research, Arn concluded, "If indeed there is a relationship between a church's quality growth and its quantity growth—that is, if loving churches do reach more people with God's love, and thus grow—then we would be good stewards to encourage a growth in quality among our churches."[9] He suggests several considerations for church leaders and their congregations:

1. *The church should make love its first priority.* Nothing is more important to the purpose of a local church than to follow Christ's command to love: To love each other, love the new member, love the visitor, love the unchurched person, love the neighbor in need. When love is a priority, a church becomes an open channel so that God's love can be expressed and experienced.

2. *The church should be a community of love.* The local congregation should be the best place to find authentic love in abundance. Regrettably, there are fraternal organizations, service clubs, even neighborhood bars where more love is found than in some churches. However, a church that claims to be Christ's body on earth must be a community of love, love that is caring, demonstrable, unconditional, and available to all who need it.

3. *A church will become more loving when its members become more loving.* The local church, as the body of Christ, is comprised of individual members. When these members learn to be vessels of Christ's love to those around them, the entire body will effectively demonstrate that love. But can people become more loving? The apostle Paul must have thought so when

he told the Corinthians to "follow the way of love" (1 Cor. 14:1).

4. *Love is the means of fulfilling the Great Commission.* The overarching priorities of Christ's followers are the Great Commandment and the Great Commission. The Great Commandment is capsuled in Mark 12:30–31: "'Love the Lord your God with all your heart and with all your soul and with all your mind and with all your strength.' The second is this: 'Love your neighbor as yourself.' There is no commandment greater than these."

The Great Commission is summarized in Matthew 28:19–20: "Therefore go and make disciples of all nations, baptizing them in the name of the Father and of the Son and of the Holy Spirit, and teaching them to obey everything I have commanded you."

As we seek to prioritize the life of our church community around the priorities of Christ's life, we find that the Great Commission—to make disciples—and the Great Commandment—to love—are inseparably linked, two sides of the same coin. The mission Christ gave us is to make disciples. The model he gave us is to love. The method is love. The motive is love. The message is love."[10]

We choose to love and forgive people because God has forgiven us of so much and has demonstrated his love to us. Jesus said, "He who has been forgiven little loves little" (Luke 7:47). But all of us have been forgiven of much, so we ought to "love much." The love we communicate and demonstrate is different than any human love. Only Christians can have this kind of compassion, commitment, and care for a world full of people who cannot naturally know God's love. John writes:

Dear friends, let us love one another, for love comes from God. Everyone who loves has been born of God and knows God. Whoever does not love does not know God, because God is love. This is how God showed his love among us: He sent his one and only Son into the world that we might live through him. This is love: not that we loved God, but that he loved us and sent his Son as an atoning sacrifice for our sins. Dear friends, since God so loved us, we also ought to love one another. No one has ever seen God; but if we love one another, God lives in us and his love is made complete in us (1 John 4:7–12).

I have always been taken aback with the history of division between black and white churches. Of all people, Christians ought to find ways to be unified. In Christianity, color, language, culture, age, education, and income make no difference. We are all one in Christ. In October 1994 I had the opportunity to be a part of what some have called the Memphis Miracle. During the meeting, leaders from various denominations began washing the feet of leaders from other denominational groups. Black leaders washed the feet of white leaders. White leaders washed the feet of black leaders. Leaders genuinely confessed their prejudices and repented in front of the crowd. Brokenness and weeping were common throughout the meeting. There was a unique presence of the Lord in the room as one person went to another and verbalized the sincere desire to be one in Christ. Out of that meeting a new multiracial, multidenominational fellowship was formed. I know this action of repentance and unity was pleasing to God and in fact was an answer to the prayer of Jesus: "Holy Father, protect them by the power of your name—the name you gave me—*so that they may be one as we are one*" (John 17:11, italics added).

Tradition tells us that the first-century pagans watched the members of the early church and said, "Behold, how they love one another!" But by the time of the reign of the emperor Julian (361–63), the situation had changed; and the pagans could honestly say, "Behold, how they fight one another!" According to the fourth-century historian Ammianus Marcellinus, the emperor "had learned that the hatred of wild beasts for man is less than the ferocity of most Christians toward one another."[11]

For too long the church has been an example of division to a world that desperately needs to know Jesus Christ. Even though I understand why different denominations have been formed and why various Christian groups have different doctrinal foundations, we must determine to be unified. For certain, we can agree on this: Jesus Christ is our Savior, "who wants all men to be saved and to come to the knowledge of the truth. For there is one God and one mediator between God and men, the man Christ Jesus, who gave himself as a ransom for all men" (1 Tim. 2:4–6).

In his book *Being a Child of God*, Warren Wiersbe reminds us of this basic but seemingly difficult truth:

> The kind of love that edifies the church isn't mere human love that enables us to get along with the people we like. It's divine love that enables us to care for and work with people we may not like. Loving only those we like and who like us will manufacture a clique, but loving all of God's people and serving them will build a church. Remember, Christian love means we treat one another the way God treats us; and God receives all of His children and accepts us in Christ. Although He has His intimates, He doesn't play favorites.[12]

The world is looking for a love that is different. They need to see the love of God in the way we choose to treat each other in the church and the way we reach out to those outside the church.

⤙ Six ⤚

Paradise Lost

I T'S COMING! ONE MADE IT THROUGH!" The young sailors from the *USS. California* screamed as a kamikaze plane streaked through the air toward their ship.

Each of the fighter jets carried two five-hundred-pound bombs. Their wings were full of gasoline, and the cockpit was sealed shut. The Japanese pilots thought that dying for their country, in this way, meant sure entry into heaven. Within seconds the kamikaze suicide mission ended with an explosion on the ship that served as home to hundreds of young sailors. A ball of flame roared across the deck. The noise was deafening; the heat scorching and deadly.

Gordy Frederick smelled the raw gas and gasped as he was blown from the gun quad onto the deck. Moments before, he had spoken to other crew members. Now no one from his quad breathed, except Gordy. His buddies, a fine-tuned team of men, were suddenly swept into eternity. Sixty-three men died because of that one plane.

Gordy lay on the deck while his lungs throbbed with excruciating pain. His clothes were burned off; his eyes swollen shut; his mouth, face, and neck badly scorched. Flames and confusion were all around him. Men frantically worked to determine who was alive. Others fought to put out the flames and stabilize the huge ship. He lay there wondering what would happen. Would they get to him in time? "At least I'm alive," he thought.

The nightmare, that would remain with him for days, had begun. Over and over he heard crew members check the fallen bodies for signs of life.

"He's dead."

"No pulse here."

"This one's dead."

When a medic checked his pulse something was terribly wrong. Gordy couldn't move, speak, or communicate in any way. Expecting to hear the medic yell for help, he heard the dreaded, hopeless words . . .

"This guy's dead."

He couldn't believe it when his dog tags were taken from his neck and tied around his ankle. This was the signal to others that his body had been checked and had no life.

Panic that Gordy had never felt before overwhelmed him as he heard someone say, "Roll him over on his face."

With all he had within, he tried to scream, "I'm not dead!"

Terror and fear enveloped him. He lay on his stomach and face with the thought rushing through his mind that surely someone would notice him. But it only got more hopeless when some time later a sailor picked him up and carried him to the makeshift morgue where the dead were temporarily being stored.

Ships are not prepared to house such a large group of dead people. The sophisticated piece of military hardware was meant to house well-trained sailors and rugged Marines. It was designed to protect them and their allies and, when necessary, destroy the enemy with incredible force. People periodically die aboard ship but not dozens of them.

A space was chosen that could be shut off from the crew, and the bodies were stacked three high. Gordy was laid on top of a dead sailor and soon another was laid on top of him. Shock overwhelmed him. He drifted in and out of consciousness as he lay in the temporary graveyard. The pain was unbearable; he could not move or see but could only hear his heart pounding in the silence of a room full of dead men.

Gordy knew that back in Tacoma, Washington, he had two dedicated Christian parents who prayed for him every day. He had run from God, but his mother and father never gave up on him. He shrugged off their attempts to reach him and pray with him, but now he desperately wanted God to hear their prayers. "God, . . . if you're real, please hear my mom and dad."

Three days later he heard the door to the room open. He could sense the light and heard some crew members come into the room. It was their job to clean up the dead men below deck. Body bags in hand, they slid each bag under the feet of a corpse. They pulled each bag to the waist then stood the stiff body up to slide it into the bag.

Gordy thought, "It's over; I can't tell them I'm alive. Once I'm in that bag no one will know."

He felt the bag slip under his ankles and up to his waist. Like the others, the sailors picked him up expecting him to be stiff from rigor mortis. When they stood him up he bent over and fell to the deck.

"Medic, Medic!" someone yelled.

The medic felt Gordy Frederick's pulse. "He's got a pulse!"

Several sailors rushed him to sick bay. He was in so much pain that he couldn't lie on a bed, but in spite of the pain, he felt overwhelmed with relief and gratitude. Doctors frantically worked on him, cleaning his throat and eyes with swabs. For the first time in days he could see blurry images. He had sustained third-degree burns over his entire body.

Gordy healed quickly, quickly enough to see further duty in the Navy. As his body recovered, he thought about the times he attended Sunday School as a child. The teachers taught him how to pray, and he thought that somehow God must be involved in all that he had gone through.

Later, Gordy completely dedicated his life to Jesus Christ. Today he bears no visible scars and has a tremendous Christian family who is involved in their local church.

For three days Gordy was forced to think about death. Over and over again, he considered where he would go if it wasn't discovered that he was alive. Was the Christian message that he had heard as a child and watched lived out through his parents, true? He thought, "I won't even have a chance to say any last words."

Have you ever thought about people's dying words? Like most of us, there have probably been few, if any, times you have permitted yourself to do this. We are not comfortable talking about death. Many people do not permit themselves to talk about the possibilities of what happens after death, especially if they feel there is a good chance they will not go to the place the Bible calls heaven. But, avoid it as we may, death will happen to every one of us.

When Thomas Paine faced death he said, "Stay with me! Stay with me, for God's sake! I cannot bear to be left alone!"

Shortly before his death, the antagonist of Christianity Voltaire said, "O Christ! O Lord Jesus, I must die—abandoned by God and men."

A. T. Adams said, "I can see the old devil in the bedroom!"

Hobbs said, "I am taking a fearful leap into the dark!"

Sir Francis Newport came to this conclusion at the end of his life: "What argument is there now to assist me against matters of fact? Do I assert there is no hell while I feel one in my own bosom? That there is a God I know, because I continually feel the effect of his wrath. That there is a hell, I am equally certain, having received an earnest of my inheritance already in my own breast."[1]

How many people live with a nagging fear about what will happen to them when they die? How many look at the world situation and have tremendous anxiety about the future? Some discuss the Y2K scare—when many computers and equipment, appliances, machines, and vehicles containing microchips may fail to operate normally after the rollover into the new millennium—and make incredible statements predicting possible worldwide chaos and anarchy. So many people live in fear. We who know Christ can have a unique peace in the middle of the storm. God does not want us to live in confusion; he wants us to be certain about our eternal future.

The God of the Bible is not hard, uncaring, and distant; rather, he is personally interested in every human being. Most people search constantly for truth and a better life. God desires that everyone know the truth through his Son Jesus Christ (1 Tim. 2:4–5) and live fulfilling lives (see John 10:10). But God is also a God of judgment and wrath, attributes that upset and confuse many people. They may say, "If God is a God of love, how can he judge people and send them to an eternal hell? How can he have wrath toward people?" Possibly the reason that many do not understand God's judgment and wrath is because they think God acts like a sinful human. When we become angry we often think, say, or do something sinful, such as "acting out" in selfish or mean ways. We may try to get back at someone for something he or she has done to us or for something we perceive he or she has done to us. God is not like us. His wrath and anger are pure. In order to be true and just, God must uphold the moral law of the universe and punish sin.

Genesis gives us a biblical view of humans and an understanding of God's wrath. The first three chapters tell us that humans are unique in that they are made in the "image of God" (Gen. 1:27). In C. S. Lewis's novel *Perelandra,* he writes about a hero named Ransom. Ransom finds himself on an uncorrupted planet called Perelandra. Sin has not affected Perelandra, so it is in the state God intended it to be from the time of its creation. At the end of the book, Ransom finally sees Adam and Eve together after their defeat of the tempter. Their appearance and presence are absolutely magnificent. Ransom is in awe of their beauty and falls to the ground in an act of worship. Why? When he saw the man and woman without the stain of sin on their lives, they looked so much like God that Ransom could hardly tell the difference. We often brush over the Scripture that tells us that God made humans in his image; this unfathomable act of our Creator needs to be remembered. What beauty, purity, strength, courage, and maturity Adam and Eve had before their decision to disobey God. The downward spiral in which we have fallen since the first couple yielded to the tempter is astonishing. When Adam and Eve rebelled against God, sin separated them from God (see Gen. 3). Spiritual alienation began at that moment.

God planned to build a wonderful world with the people he had created. He made man and woman to have fellowship with him. Humans were to live in peace and dignity and were to continually sense their Creator's presence. But look at what we have today. In the newspaper we see scandal, murder, hatred, and economic despair. On the nightly news we see warring nations, devastating famine, incurable illnesses, and corrupt government leaders. All of this is attributable to humankind's spiritual rebellion against God. Because of sin, humans have traded spiritual life for spiritual death.

Through Jesus, God has provided eternal life for those who know him; however, his wrath is eternal death for those who choose to reject him. Scripture tells us, "Just as sin entered the world through one man, and death through sin, and in this way death came to all men, because all sinned" (Rom. 5:12).

"Life" means more than just our physical life; our existence— sense of being, presence, and who we are—will go on for eternity after physical death. "Whoever believes in the Son has eternal life, but whoever rejects the Son will not see life, for God's wrath remains on him" (John 3:36). God created us to enjoy eternal life with him—a relationship with God here and now as well as in heaven. Eternal death means that we lose the kind of life God created us to have. It is more than physical dissolution—it is a loss of the relationship and fellowship that God desires to have with us for eternity.

What Is Hell?

IN HIS CLASSIC BOOK *The Screwtape Letters*, C. S. Lewis provides a series of imaginary letters that demons write to each other in their quest to distract people from God. In one letter the demons write:

> Encourage in your own minds that delusion which you must carefully foster in the minds of your human victims. I mean

the delusion that the fate of nations is *in itself* more important than that of individual souls. The overthrow of free
peoples and the multiplication of slave states are for us a
means (besides, of course, being fun); but the real end is the
destruction of individuals. For only individuals can be saved
or damned, can become sons of the Enemy or food for us.
The ultimate value, for us, of any revolution, war, or famine
lies in the individual anguish, treachery, hatred, rage, and
despair which it may produce. *I'm as good as you* is a useful
means for the destruction of democratic societies. But it has
a far deeper value as an end in itself, as a state of mind which,
necessarily excluding humility, charity, contentment, and all
the pleasures of gratitude or admiration, turns a human
being away from almost every road which might finally lead
him to Heaven.[2]

Satan does not care what tactic is used to keep people from
knowing God. He is involved in guerrilla warfare and will use
whatever means he can to distract people from a relationship with
Jesus Christ.

The fast, pounding, confusing, and hateful music of Marilyn
Manson might disgust us, but he and his music have become fads
with thousands of young people throughout the world. He is an
example of how the enemy of our souls can carefully weave a web
of confusion, hurt, and bitterness in a person's life. One of his most
popular CDs is *Antichrist Superstar*. Born in a dream Manson
claims to have had, the CD explores the transformation and meta-
morphosis of a worm into an angel and then into a world-destroying demon. Manson sees the story as autobiographical. The worm
was Brian Warner (Manson's real name). The world-destroying
demon is his newest persona: the antichrist superstar/a pop icon on
a mission to encourage people to question the existence of God and
believe only in themselves.[3] In the opening song of the CD, a crowd
chants, "We love hate. We hate love...." As the song plays, Manson
screams, "Let's just kill everyone and let God sort them out."[4]

I have often wondered what makes some people hate so
much. Is there something painful in the background of people like

Hitler, Lenin, Mussolini, and Ceausescu? How did Marilyn Manson become what he is? There is no question that he has chosen his behavior and his lucrative career; but beneath all the makeup, vulgarity, and bold performance is a man who has incredible insecurity and painful memories. Walt Mueller, president of the Center for Parent/Youth Understanding, has written:

> Underneath the makeup is a man who was born Brian Warner in Canton, Ohio. His father was a furniture salesman who Manson says was rarely home. Skinny and sickly, Manson was the friendless schoolyard whipping boy.
>
> A series of strange events left a lasting mark on the boy. At age 8, an 11-year-old neighbor boy repeatedly convinced Brian to play a "game" that required him to take off his clothes. The boy would run his hands all over Warner's body. Then, at age 13, he discovered his grandfather in an indecent situation and later discovered that his grandfather was obsessed with hardcore pornography and female clothing. Manson says those experiences stole part of his childhood: "In many ways my desire is actually to be pure again and not dirtied by the world. But I feel it's my duty to be as ugly and filthy as I am ... so the audience can experience what I've experienced. It's cathartic" (*Details* magazine, December 1996).
>
> In 1974 Manson's parents enrolled him in a Christian school where years of religious instruction took the form of discussions, movies and Bible studies on the coming apocalypse that left him trembling with fear that the world would end, he wouldn't go to heaven, and he'd never see his parents again. "It was then that I began having nightmares—nightmares that continue to this day," writes Manson in his autobiography *The Long Hard Road Out of Hell* (HarperCollins). "I was thoroughly terrified by the idea of the end of the world and the Antichrist. . . . What if I already had the mark of the beast on me? . . . What if the Antichrist was me? I was filled with fear and confusion at a time when, even without the influence of Christian school, I was already in turmoil because I was going through puberty." To this day, Manson can't go to sleep without the TV on as background noise.

Because his home life seemed so different from the Christian students, Manson felt like he stood out, especially when there was a public call for commitment. "Every time I knew I should have walked up there, but I was too petrified to stand on-stage in front of the entire school and too embarrassed to admit that I was morally, spiritually and religiously behind everyone else." In an attempt to fit in, Manson brought in one of his favorite possessions to share with his fourth-grade class. It was a photograph his grandmother had taken of a cloud formation in which there appeared to be an angel. His teachers called it a hoax; he was scolded and sent home for being blasphemous. Deeply hurt, he remembers it as "my most honest attempt to fit in with their idea of Christianity, to prove my connection with their beliefs, and I was punished for it." That same year, a drama teacher cast him as Jesus in a school play. After the crucifixion scene, he went backstage wearing the loincloth costume. Several older kids ripped it off, whipped him with it, and chased him naked down the corridor in front of his classmates.

When Manson was 18, his family moved to Fort Lauderdale, Florida, and in 1989 he founded the band "Marilyn Manson and the Spooky Kids.".... At the end of the first show he says, "I heard applause, and suddenly I felt something rise inside me.... It was a sense of pride, accomplishment and self satisfaction strong enough to eclipse my withering self-image and my punching-bag past. It was the first time in my life I felt that way. And I wanted to feel like that again."[5]

As Paul Harvey says, "And now, you know the rest of the story."

We look at Manson and are disgusted, offended, and possibly enraged about what he is trying to do to young people. There is no question that we should be greatly concerned and, in fact, should protect our young people from seeing or hearing him. But we must recognize the root cause of his radical behavior, blasphemous verbiage, and hatred of Christianity. Looking back, we can see how Satan endeavored to keep Brian Warner from the truth. He was a targeted young man. Everyone is. You and I are. Satan wants to populate hell.

Hell was not created for people; it was created for the devil and his angels (Matt. 25:41). This place is not the place that people call "hell on earth" when they're having a bad day or going through a tough situation. When people say that I often think, "They have no idea what hell is like, because if they did, they wouldn't use the name in that way." God did not create hell to scare people. It is a real location and any being (fallen angel or human) who goes there will stay there for eternity.

The concept of hell is not exclusive to the Christian faith. In his book *Facing Death and the Life After,* Billy Graham writes, "Centuries before Christ, the Babylonians believed in 'The Land of No-Return.' The Hebrews wrote about going down to the realm of Sheol, or the place of corruption; the Greeks spoke of the 'Unseen Land.' Classical Buddhism recognizes seven 'hot hells,' and the Hindu *Rig Veda* speaks of the deep abyss reserved for false men and faithless women. Islam recognizes seven hells."[6]

Hell is not a popular subject. If a pastor preaches on hell, he is criticized for preaching too much "fire and brimstone." If we talk about hell, we may be called extremists. Religions have been created in order to avoid the subject. Universalism teaches that eventually everyone will be saved because God would never send anyone to hell. Universalists believe that the words "eternal" or "everlasting" do not actually mean forever. The same word that speaks of eternal banishment from God, however, is also used for the eternity in heaven.[7] Universalism is wrong and in fact danger-ous, because there *is* an eternal hell, and this religion is deceiving people by telling them that no one could go there. After physical death there are no second chances. The doctrine of purgatory is unbiblical. After death people do not remain in a state of "limbo" working themselves back into right relationship with God. After death it's over. That is why we must remind people that today is the day of salvation (2 Cor. 6:2). We have no guarantees about tomorrow.

Hell is a place of incredible sorrow and torment, "the fiery furnace, where there will be weeping and gnashing of teeth" (Matt. 13:42). Hell is a place of eternal fire: "Then death and Hades were thrown into the lake of fire. The lake of fire is the second death" (Rev. 20:14).

After physical death, the eternal destiny for those who are without Christ is terrible. The Bible tells us that "It would be better for him if he had not been born" (Matt. 26:24). "The smoke of their torment rises for ever and ever. There is no rest day or night" (Rev. 14:11). Paul speaks of "everlasting destruction" (2 Thess. 1:9), and Peter speaks of "gloomy dungeons" (2 Peter 2:4).

Billy Graham has written:

> Will a loving God send a man to hell? The answer from Jesus and the teachings of the Bible is, clearly, "Yes!" He does not send man willingly, but man condemns himself to eternal hell. Because of man's blindness, stubbornness, egotism, and love of sinful pleasure, he refuses God's way of salvation and the hope of eternal life with him.
>
> Suppose a person is sick and goes to a doctor. The doctor diagnoses the problem and prescribes medicine. However, the advice is ignored and in a few days the person stumbles back into the doctor's office and says, "It's your fault that I'm worse. Do something."
>
> God has prescribed the remedy for spiritual sickness of the human race. The solution is personal faith and commitment to Jesus Christ. Since the remedy is to be born again, if we deliberately refuse it, we must suffer the horrible consequences.[8]

God does not want anyone to go to hell. He desires everyone to be saved (1 Tim. 2:4). His love is big enough to include everyone (John 3:16). But people can choose to reject God's offer and spend eternity away from his presence and his kingdom.

In his classic book *Paradise Lost*, John Milton described hell.

A dungeon Horrible on all sides round,
As one great furnace, flamed; yet from those flames

No light, but rather darkness visible
Serv'd only to discover sights of woe,
Regions of sorrow, soleful shades, where peace
And rest can never dwell, hope never comes
That comes to all; but torture without end.[9]

Leaders in the early church were very aware of the future of those who rejected the gospel and lived in sin. They preached with tears (Acts 20:19) and passionately defended God's Word and the true gospel of Jesus Christ against all aberrational teaching and heresy. We should do no less. Perhaps the greatest motivation for telling others about Christ is the possibility that they could spend eternity in hell. We need to think about our relatives, our friends, those we work with and live around. Where will they spend eternity? The realization of heaven and hell ought to motivate us to do all we can to help people go to heaven. You could be the only missionary in their lives. This thought might seem overwhelming to you, but the life you live in front of others, and the words and Scriptures you choose to witness to people, will be used by the Holy Spirit to speak to people about their eternal destinies. In his book *Evangelism that Works*, George Barna lists several practical truths about effective evangelism.

- The message is God's. The means of getting the message to those who need to hear it is by people communicating that message through words and actions that are consistent with the lessons in the Bible.
- God can, has and will use anybody who is open to serving Him to convey the gospel. He will bless the efforts of His servants whether they are gifted as evangelizers or not.
- We are called to take advantage of opportunities to share our faith in Christ and to make the most of those opportunities. However, the act of converting a person from condemned sinner to forgiven and loved disciple of Christ is the job of the Holy Spirit. The evangelizer plays a role in the conversion process but will not be

held accountable for the choice made by those who hear the gospel.

- The most powerful attraction to a nonbeliever is seeing the life of someone transformed by the reality of the gospel. Although a verbal explanation of that faith is helpful toward facilitating a nonbeliever's decision to follow Christ, a verbal proclamation without a lifestyle that supports that proclamation is powerless.
- The most effective evangelists are the most obedient and committed Christians. They need not have formal theological training, a full-time position in a church or credentials such as ordination. They need a passion for Christ, a desire to make Him known to the world and the willingness to be used in any and all situations to help usher others into the kingdom of God.
- Evangelism is the bridge we build between our love for God and our love for other people. Through the work of the Holy Spirit, through us, God can complete his transformation of a person for his purposes and glory.
- We cannot give away what we don't have. Therefore, we must be in close relationship with God and must be open to being used by Him as a conduit of His grace.
- Effective outreach always involves sincere and fervent prayer that God will bless those efforts, although there is no guarantee of the nonbeliever making the right choice.
- Knowing, trusting and using God's Word is central to leading a person to a lifesaving faith in Jesus.
- When we intelligently share our faith with nonbelievers, it pleases God.
- Every Christian must be ready at all times and in all situations to share his or her faith in Christ with those who do not have a relationship with Christ.
- Evangelism is not meant to be limited by human convenience or preference. It is to be done with obedience and faith.
- The most effective evangelistic efforts are those that are simple and sincere.

- Evangelism that starts at the nonbeliever's point of felt need and ties the gospel into that area of need has the greatest capacity for capturing the mind and heart of the non-Christian.
- Outreach efforts that take advantage of the credibility, accessibility and trust of an existing friendship have a better chance of succeeding than does "cold call" evangelism. However, God uses all sincere and appropriate attempts to serve Him and to love others by sharing the gospel.[10]

What Is Heaven?

PHILIP YANCEY WROTE A strange fact about modern American life: "Although 71 percent of us believe in an afterlife (says George Gallup), no one much talks about it. Christians believe that we will spend eternity in a splendid place called heaven.... Isn't it a little bizarre that we simply ignore heaven, acting as if it doesn't matter?"[11]

Many people do not think about heaven because it is difficult to imagine, especially in a Western culture where there is so much affluence and material wealth. We can advance educationally, occupationally, and materially, and have relatively little reason to want to go somewhere else. This comfort with earthly things could be our greatest danger. The early church looked forward with great anticipation to the time when they would go to heaven. Christians are aliens on this earth; we have another home. We belong to God's kingdom, not the kingdom of this world.

Years ago, Elisabeth Kübler-Ross wrote about the five stages of death. This philosophy is commonly taught in hospitals, universities, and even some religious institutions. She taught that one of the most healthy stages is the "acceptance" stage. If a dying person, or the loved one of the dying person, comes to this stage, that person will be "healthier." I have often thought, *What if the person is not a Christian? If we convince this person to accept his or her state, then we could be a participant in the Enemy's strategy to keep the person from wanting Christ and going to heaven.*

Philip Yancey said, "I have watched in hospital groups as dying patients worked desperately toward a calm stage of acceptance. Strangely, no one ever talked about heaven in those groups; it seemed embarrassing, somehow cowardly. What convulsion of values can have us holding up the prospect of annihilation as brave and that of blissful eternity as cowardly?"[12]

No matter how eloquent a person's human language is, it will always fall short when trying to describe heaven. In fact, I'm not sure that we can ever understand heaven's wonder and majesty until we finally get there. The Bible tells us that:

Heaven is a place where the perfect presence of God dwells and everyone who knows him will be there. I love to study the heroes of the faith—from those we read about in Scripture, like Noah, Abraham, Moses, David, Esther, Daniel, Mary, Joseph, John, and Paul, to those who have been greatly used of God since the inception of the church. We will spend eternity with these people.

There are no denominations in heaven. Wayde and I are part of the Assemblies of God fellowship. We love the fellowship we belong to. In heaven, however, there will be no Assemblies of God corner nor Baptist, Presbyterian, Methodist, Catholic or whatever denomination you might be part of. We are all in God's church when we belong to Jesus Christ; and when we get to heaven, the denomination we belonged to on this earth will make absolutely no difference. The only thing that will matter is that we belong to Jesus.

In heaven we will clearly understand. There is much we do not understand on this earth—governments, scientific knowledge, creation, angels, tragedy, pain and suffering, to list a few. In this life we listen to teachers, pastors, writers, philosophers, and employers. In heaven we will be in the presence of the Creator of the universe, the source of all wisdom and knowledge. The term *enlightened* is often used by religious groups to describe understanding. In heaven we will most certainly be enlightened. John tells us that "God is light; in him there is no darkness at all" (1 John 1:5). He also informs us that we can "walk in the light" (1 John 1:7). David asked, "The LORD is my light and my salvation—whom shall I fear?" (Ps. 27:1). Light is a symbol of understanding. In heaven God's perfect light will push away any darkness.

In heaven there will be no more pain, no more death, no more sickness and suffering. John wrote, "And I heard a loud voice from the throne saying, 'Now the dwelling of God is with men, and he will live with them. They will be his people, and God himself will be with them and be their God. He will wipe every tear from their eyes. There will be no more death or mourning or crying or pain, for the old order of things has passed away'" (Rev. 21:3–5).

Heaven is where people who know Jesus Christ as their personal Savior will go. More than anything this world could offer (fame, power, or security), I want my family, my friends, and everyone else my life touches to go to heaven. The thought of someone spending eternity in hell sickens me. The thought of people repenting, giving their lives to Christ, and spending eternity in heaven thrills me.

Losing a loved one can be hard, even when that loved one is going to heaven. One of the most difficult things a pastor does is to comfort family members after they have lost someone they love, especially when that person is a child. Children are supposed to bury parents, not the other way around.

One Sunday afternoon I was called at home and informed of a tragedy that had happened with one of the teenagers in our church. It seems that some of the young people had gone swimming that day, and because the park was full of people and many in the youth group were coming and going, the kids didn't keep an eye on each other. When they decided to get something to eat, they noticed Tad was missing. They looked all over the park, thinking he went for a walk. Then they decided to look for his car. It was there and his dry clothing was inside. They were fearful of the worst. The park was cleared and the fire department was called. It didn't take long to find Tad's body. The police suspected that he had been too tired to make it to the dock and drowned.

Tad was an extraordinary young man. He was mentally gifted and had a difficult time making friends until he started attending the church's youth group about a year before his death. When he found kids who liked him and included him, he showed up at just about everything the church had to offer. He attended all the services, youth programs, and even the small Saturday night prayer meetings. He would often come up to me at the prayer meeting and share something about his newfound faith in Jesus Christ. Tad also told as many people as he could about his faith.

As I sat at his parents' dining room table, we all wept and talked about Tad. Tad's successful father was not a Christian but deeply respected his son's faith. During the last year, Tad's father had even taken extra time off work (several months) to spend time with Tad before Tad left for college. They had a tremendous relationship. The father was overwhelmed because not only was Tad his only child, he was also his dear friend.

The father said to me, "Pastor, what tears me apart is that I will never see Tad again. I can't handle that thought."

I responded to him, "Sir, you *can* see your son again. As sure as I am sitting here, I know where Tad is at this moment." I added, "You have spent so much time with him during these last months, and you know how much his faith in Christ meant to him. The Bible that Tad faithfully read (his Bible was sitting right there on the table) tells us that there is a heaven, and that is where Tad is."

Tad's dad said, "I want to go where my son is." We then prayed, and he asked Christ to forgive him of his sins and to take control of his life. Every Sunday, Wednesday, and Saturday I saw Tad's dad. He carried his son's Bible and would often show me a verse that Tad had underlined, saying, "Look at this verse: Tad loved this one." He began to grow in Christ and wanted everything God had to offer. One day he will be reunited with Tad. More than that, he will spend eternity in heaven with everyone who knows Christ.[13]

~⇒ SEVEN ⇐~

God's Strategic Plan

I N THE HISTORIC CONFERENCE called the Lausanne Congress on
World Evangelization, Billy Graham said:

> I believe there are two strains in prophetic Scripture.
> One leads us to understand that as we approach the latter
> days and the Second Coming of Christ, things will become
> worse and worse. Joel speaks of "multitudes, multitudes in
> the valley of decision!" The day of the Lord is near in the val-
> ley of decision. He is speaking of judgment.
>
> But I believe as we approach the latter days and the
> coming of the Lord, it could be a time also of great revival.
> We cannot forget the possibility and the promise of revival,
> the refreshing of the latter days of the outpouring of the
> Spirit promised in Joel 2:28 and repeated in Acts 2:17. That
> will happen right up to the advent of the Lord Jesus Christ.
>
> Evil will grow worse, but God will be mightily at work
> at the same time. I am praying that we will see in the next
> months and years the "latter rains," a rain of blessings, show-
> ers falling from heaven upon all the continents before the
> coming of the Lord.[1]

Ministry Advantage of Fuller Theological Seminary reported
the following marvelous statistics concerning revival in the world:

> Almost every continent has experienced a massive
> revival of Christianity in recent years. Around the world
> Christianity is growing at an amazing rate—an estimated
> 178,000 people are receiving Christ daily. An estimated

28,000 are coming to Christ in China daily, 20,000 in Africa, and 35,000 in Latin America. Some 3,000 new churches are opening every week worldwide.

Christianity is the fastest-growing religious movement in the world, with a 6.9% growth rate.

- China—In 1950 China had 1 million believers. By 1980 there were 40 million believers. Today there are as many as 100 million.
- Russia—After 70 years of oppression, people who are officially Christians number about 85 million—56% of the population. In one Siberian city people are being baptized 24 hours a day.
- Africa—The southern part of Africa was 3% Christian in 1900 and is nearly 60% Christian today.
- Latin America—Latin Americans are receiving Christ at a rate that is four times faster than the population growth. In 1900 there were only 50,000 born-again believers in Latin America. By 1980 there were 20 million. By the year 2000 that number is expected to grow to more than 100 million.
- Iran—More Muslims in Iran have come to Christ since 1980 than in the previous 1,000 years combined.
- Korea—In 1900 Korea had no Protestant church. Today Korea is 35% Christian.
- Saudi Arabia—During the Persian Gulf War, more than 100 churches were planted in Saudi Arabia. Since Desert Storm, more than 3,000 Saudi Muslims have come to Christ.
- Myanmar—It's reported that 37 of the nation's top Buddhist monks gave their hearts to the Lord during presentation of the Jesus film.[2]

What a day to be alive. Never has there been such a great effort from most denominational groups throughout the world to evangelize. I have always believed that the Bible promises that there will be a major worldwide revival in the last days.[3] Author Neil Anderson said, "Globally, the Holy Spirit has woven together a massive cooperative effort that could produce a harvest of at least one billion souls in the next five years. The church could be experiencing the first fruits of the greatest awakening it has ever known."[4]

As we enter the third millennium since Christ, we could be the very people that Jesus talked about who would be alive when he returns to take true Christian believers from this earth. We could be the "terminal generation" who will actually have this experience.

The Bible tells us, "The Lord himself will come down from heaven with a loud command, with the voice of the archangel and with the trumpet call of God, and the dead in Christ will rise first. After that, we who are still alive and are left will be *caught up* together with them in the clouds to meet the Lord in the air. And so we will be with the Lord forever" (1 Thess. 4:16–17, italics added).

Think about it. Christian believers from all over the world and from all walks of life will one day experience this event. The Bible tells us two will be working together, and one will be taken and the other left (see Matt. 24:40–41). Christian leaders, pilots, taxi-cab drivers, factory workers, politicians, salespeople, engineers, mechanics, doctors, lawyers, housewives—people of all ages, colors, and nationalities who will suddenly be gone from the earth.

Before this occurrence, which many call the rapture, there will be no warning, no time to say I'm sorry, no last-minute repentance. This event, on God's timetable, will suddenly usher in the most terrible time of history that this world has ever experienced—the seven-year tribulation. We would never want our friends and loved ones to go through such a horrible time. In comparison, it will make the horrors of the Holocaust look mild.

The words "caught up" (Greek *harpazo*, "to seize, snatch") refer to the catching up of the church from the earth. *Rapture* comes from the Latin word *rapere*, which means "caught away or caught up." At that moment, those who have died in Christ and Christians who are living will "be changed—in a flash, in the twinkling of an eye, at the last trumpet. For the trumpet will sound, the dead will be raised imperishable, and we will be changed" (1 Cor.

15:51–52). As a Christian, you will leave the gravitational pull of the earth and suddenly meet Jesus Christ in the clouds. During that split-second time of travel, your body will change into a body that will never die.

Throughout the world people have a keen interest in last-day prophecies and events such as the rapture. Whether or not we agree with the contents or the conclusions of Hal Lindsay's predictions concerning the last days, the incredible success of his book *The Late Great Planet Earth* gives an indication of people's heightened interest in this subject. For ten years this book was the number one best-seller in the world, with the sole exception of the Bible.[5]

Jesus gave us a significant clue to when the rapture will happen. Moments before his ascension from earth to heaven, Jesus instructed his disciples saying, "You will receive power when the Holy Spirit comes on you; and you will be my witnesses in Jerusalem, and in all Judea and Samaria, and to the ends of the earth" (Acts 1:8). Before his crucifixion and death he looked down through thousands of years of history and prophesied that "this gospel of the kingdom will be preached in the whole world as a testimony to all nations, and then the end will come" (Matt. 24:14). *"You will be my witnesses,"* has been being fulfilled for almost two thousand years, and now we are poised with the very real possibility that the *whole world* could hear the gospel—"then the end will come."

Jesus did not say exactly when he would come back. Those who set specific dates are not being attentive to what Scripture tells us. Jesus said, "No one knows about that day or hour, not even the angels in heaven, nor the Son, but only the Father" (Matt. 24:36). Revelation 6 gives an amazing portrait of the end times, but no one knows the timing of these events except our heavenly Father. Not even the angels know. I am sure the angels are awaiting the time when the church will be removed from this earth, but only God through his infinite knowledge will know when that last person has heard the gospel of Jesus Christ.

Even though we do not know the exact time, Jesus said there would be certain signs that we could watch for. In fact, he said, "Keep watch, because you do not know on what day your Lord will come. . . . You also must be ready" (Matt. 24:42, 44).

Watch

ONE OF THE MOST stressful occupations in the world is that of an air traffic controller. A significant percentage of people who hold this very responsible job suffer from ulcers and other physiological problems that are brought on by the constant tension that is a normal part of their day. While on duty, they must be alert, attentive, and ready to react at any time. There is little or no margin for error.

Recently the network news reported what could have been an incredible tragedy. It seems that both of the air traffic controllers who had the "middle of the night" (1:00–5:00 A.M.) shift at a midsize airport fell asleep during their watch. Since they rarely had any traffic during that time, they allowed themselves to nod off. What they didn't know was that during that time a passenger carrier had been trying to reach them to ask for permission to land at their airport, and a small plane needed to make an emergency landing. Both pilots were unable to reach anyone at the airport. Thankfully, the airplanes did find a place to land, but the situation could have ended with another horrible headline. The traffic controllers might lose their careers (or worse) in the inquiry that will follow.

In our spiritual lives, we must not nod off. We must watch, wait, and work with expectation and anticipation. Yes, about two thousand years have passed since Jesus left this earth, and many have chosen to say, "Where is this 'coming' he promised? Ever since our fathers died, everything goes on as it has since the beginning of creation" (2 Peter 3:4). But we should not feel this way. The only remaining reason that God has not taken the church from the earth is that he wants every human being to hear the gospel of Jesus Christ. He does not want anyone to go to hell. "The Lord is not slow in keeping his promise, as some understand slowness. He is patient with you, not wanting anyone to perish, but everyone to come to repentance" (2 Peter 3:9).

In his book *The Coming World Revival*, Robert Coleman writes, "The massive turning to Christ by people from the four corners of the earth will prepare the way for the coming of the King. Our Lord's return may be waiting now on this spiritual revolution."[6] "Be patient, then, brothers, until the Lord's coming. See how the farmer waits for the land to yield its valuable crop and how patient he is for the autumn and spring rains. You too, be patient and stand firm, because the Lord's coming is near" (James 5:7–8).

Christians should not be surprised by the return of Jesus Christ. We can look around the world and observe the signs and anticipate his return. Billy Graham said:

> Jesus used images that were dramatic and compelling, but He did not engage in fantasy. He told his followers, "I am the way and the truth, and the life. No one comes to the Father except through me" (John 14:6), and He was truth and veracity personified. Jesus indicated that when certain things come to pass, we can be assured that the end is near. He said, "You can read the signs of the weather in the sky, but because of spiritual blindness you cannot read the signs of the times." He indicated that only those who have spiritual illumination and discernment from the Holy Spirit can hope to understand the trends and meanings of history.[7]

As believers, we should not be surprised at Jesus' coming— that is, we should not experience his coming like a thief in the night (Matt. 24:43; cf. 1 Thess. 5:4). We should, however, have a sense that he could return at any moment. Why? Because the signs are all around this generation.

Signs to Watch For

Nature

"There will be famines and earthquakes in various places. All these are the beginning of birth pains" (Matt. 24:7). Birth pains occur more often and with greater intensity as a women gets closer to the time of her baby's birth. Likewise, famines and earthquakes will become more and more frequent and intense as we get closer to the time of Jesus' return. During the final days, more earthquakes will occur around the world, and famines will occur in spite of the abilities of farmers to produce crops.

In the *World Press Report*, Michael Ignatieff wrote, "Famine has come to Africa. Again. Twenty-six million people are at risk in Sudan, Ethiopia, Somalia, Malawi, Angola, and Mozambique. In all those places . . . civil war conspires with drought in wiping out the human race."[8]

Tonight on the evening news we could hear words similar to these of Ignatieff: "Here they come: the stick children with the flat, unseeing stares. Their knee sockets are so large, and their calves are so thin that you wonder how they manage to walk. They are too weak to sweep away the flies that have settled on their mouths and nostrils. They can only hold their bowls out toward the television cameras."[9] This is just not a picture of Cambodia or Vietnam in the 1960s, Bangladesh in the 1970s or Ethiopia in the 1980s. These words can just as easily describe an ongoing struggle in East Africa today.

With the economic instability in today's world, we could see nation after nation virtually lose the ability to buy food. The devaluation of the Russian ruble and the Mexican peso, or the financial crisis in Brazil and Indonesia or most any third-world country could cause massive famine and starvation in these nations. A news story from Mozambique said, "The problem is that money has no value here anymore. How would you like to make half what you earned twelve years ago and you still can't supply the basic needs of your family?"[10]

The World Bank reported, "Half of the people in absolute poverty lie in South Asia, mainly in India and Bangladesh. A sixth live in East and Southeast Asia. Another sixth are in sub-Saharan Africa. The rest are divided among Latin America, North Africa and the Middle East." In these southern hemisphere and tropical regions that we now commonly refer to as the third world, the United Nations estimates that at least 100 million children go to bed hungry every night.[11]

In contrast to this heart-wrenching problem, it is said that Americans spend an annual $15 billion on diet formulas and $22 billion on cosmetics.[12] The money spent on these items alone could save literally tens of thousands of people who are dying of starvation as you read this page.

At times my heart cries out, "Unfair!" At other times I am overwhelmed with gratitude that my children and grandchildren can be raised in a land such as America. We must do all that we can to help those who do not have enough food, clothing, or medical assistance. Only a few countries in the world annually produce more wheat than they consume. These include the United States, Australia, and Canada; however, adverse weather in these regions could cause these nations to lose the ability to sell as much, or any, wheat to needy nations.

Society

In our book *The Battle: Defeating the Enemies of Your Soul*, we write about signs we must look for in society. Jesus gives us many specific signs of the last days. Among them are the religion of humanism, the craving for materialism, the devotion to hedonism, and the feeling of nihilism that will invade the hearts of millions. Today we find:

Humanism is a common religion in the world. Humanism is the worship of self instead of God. People will be interested in their own welfare, values, and interests without taking God into consideration. In their selfishness to satisfy their desires, they will forget God and worship the creature rather than the Creator

(Rom. 1:22–23, 25; 2 Tim. 3:2). Even more pernicious than this egocentric way of living are religions that teach that people can actually become gods. This false concept is common in New Age teaching. Also, Mormonism teaches, "As man is, God once was, and as God is, man may become." The founder of the Mormon church said, "God was once a man like us and dwelt on an earth, the same as Jesus Christ did, and you have got to learn to be gods yourselves the same as all gods before you."

The spirit of humanism began with prideful Lucifer. He thought only of himself, and this lurid thought turned into the idea that he could be as powerful as God. Satan himself has promoted self-centered humanism.

Materialism is a common false god. People want more and more material belongings and money. Greed will increase worldwide (Rom. 1:29). . . . Satan wants us to think that our happiness, peace, contentment, and feelings of security come from what we own. In the last days this lie will deceive many into looking to material gain as the mark of success. There is no question that God often blesses his people materially and will supply their needs. But our joy and peace come from the Lord and not from what we own. All over the world there are dynamic, committed believers in Jesus Christ who have very little in earthly possessions, but give a wonderful demonstration of the blessing of God in their lives.

Hedonism is a common lifestyle. The devotion to pleasure and self-gratification, accompanied by a disregard for conventional morality, is rapidly becoming a way of life. The achievement of pleasure, no matter what the cost, is the goal of many today. The Bible states that people will be lovers of self more than lovers of God or his will (2 Tim. 3:2–4). People will try to suppress the truth about God (Rom. 1:18–22, 30). Many would like to put an end to God's Word and his truth. People will give themselves over to sexual impurity (Rom. 1:24) and become more open about homosexual behavior (vv. 26–27).

Television, movies, videos, gimmicks, and games continually promote a hedonistic attitude. They try to communicate that

Christian values and principles are old-fashioned. Their message, whether promoting immorality or denigrating religious faith, becomes bolder and bolder as we approach the end of the age.

Nihilism—despair—is a common condition. As people alienate themselves from a holy God, love will grow cold (Matt. 24:12). People will become more and more out of control because of their abuse of morality (Rom. 1:28–32). When people ignore God and his will, difficult times come (2 Tim. 3:2–4). There will be more and more violence and lawlessness. People will become more arrogant and even brag about their ungodly behavior. Mocking God and even blaspheming him will be common (see Rom. 1:30; 2 Tim. 3:2–4). Paul warned Timothy that these days would be difficult (2 Tim. 3:1).

Many will suffer because of this rejection of God's principles. There will be a rebellious spirit among children (2 Tim. 3:2), maliciousness (gossip, slander, envy, malice, vv. 2–4), deceit (Rom. 1:29, 31), betrayal by family members (Mark 13:12), stress to the point that "men will faint from terror" (Luke 21:26), and people will hate good (2 Tim. 3:3). The day will be full of despair.[13]

Think about it for a moment. When you read the newspaper or listen to the evening world report, do these signs stand out? They are all around us.

Religion

"At that time if anyone says to you, 'Look, here is the Christ!' or, 'There he is!' do not believe it. For false Christs and false prophets will appear and perform great signs and miracles to deceive even the elect—if that were possible" (Matt. 24:23–24).

As we watch the world of religion, we will see both negative spiritual occurrences and positive spiritual growth. On the negative side we will hear of false Christs and of the multiplication of cults. Apostasy will be common in the church, and persecution of Christians will increase worldwide. Interest in the paranormal, the worship of Satan, and the occult will dramatically increase as well. Many portions of Scripture warn us of this time:

The Spirit clearly says that in later times some will abandon the faith and follow deceiving spirits. (1 Tim. 4:1)

But mark this: There will be terrible times in the last days. People will be lovers of themselves, lovers of money, boastful, proud, abusive, disobedient to their parents, ungrateful, unholy, without love, unforgiving, slanderous, without self-control, brutal, not lovers of the good, treacherous, rash, conceited, lovers of pleasure rather than lovers of God—having a form of godliness but denying its power. (2 Tim. 3:1–5)

But there were also false prophets among the people, just as there will be false teachers among you. They will secretly introduce destructive heresies, even denying the sovereign Lord who bought them. (2 Peter 2:1–2)

You must understand that in the last days scoffers will come, scoffing and following their own evil desires. (2 Peter 3:3)

Dear children, this is the last hour; and as you have heard that the antichrist is coming, even now many antichrists have come. This is how we know it is the last hour. (1 John 2:18)

Billy Graham said,

We have seen moral and religious leaders, men who claim to be followers of Jesus, fall into disgrace in the eyes of God and man. And worst of all, we have seen the gospel of Jesus Christ twisted and distorted by false teachers to accommodate the destructive morals and secular behavior of these times. These warnings from the Book of Matthew are not parables or myths; they are the very headlines of our day. They are the evidence of Christ's prophecy fulfilled before our eyes.

But the true church would grow through persecution, Jesus said. It would spring forth from darkness and neglect even as the churches of Romania, Bulgaria, and East Germany have sprung full-blown from the soil of despair. "And this gospel of the kingdom will be preached in all the world as a witness to all the nations," He told them, "and then the end will come."[14]

As we mentioned earlier in this chapter and in chapter 4, the positive religious signs we watch for are all around us as well. Robert Coleman said,

> The coming world revival will naturally result in multitudes calling upon the name of the Lord for salvation (Joel 2:32; Acts 2:21; cf. Rom. 10:13). And the same revival will also prepare workers for that great harvest of souls. People full of the Holy Spirit are committed to God's work. They want to be where laborers are needed most, and there is no more pressing need than bringing the gospel to hell-bound men and women.
>
> Significantly, Jesus said that the fulfillment of his preaching mission would precede his return: "This gospel of the Kingdom will be preached in the whole world as a testimony to all nations, and then the end will come" (Matt. 24:14; cf. Luke 12:36–37; 14:15–23). Doubtless the passion to get out the message while there is yet time will increase with the revival, even as the witnesses multiply. That the gospel will eventually penetrate "every nation, tribe, people and language" is clear from the description of the innumerable throng of God in heaven (Rev. 7:9; cf. 5:9). The Great Commission will finally be fulfilled.[15]

Never in the history of the church has the gospel been advanced as it is today. I can't help but think of the Protestant denomination that Wayde and I are a part of. It began in 1914 with just a few and today has nearly 30 million people. We are a part of what has been called Pentecostalism. In the book *The Life Millennium: The 100 Most Important Events and People of the Past 1,000 Years*, the writers at Time/Life report,

> Pentecostalism is a religion of the heart. Since a personal experience is as important as doctrine, it is an adaptable faith; by the end of the 1960s Protestants and Catholics had both begun to embrace the gifts of the Spirit in Charismatic renewal movements.... Today about half a billion people call themselves Pentecostal or Charismatic, and Pentecostals

alone outnumber Anglicans, Baptists, Lutherans and Pres-
byterians combined. The Yoido Full Gospel Church in
Seoul, South Korea, is now at 700,000 strong, the largest
Christian congregation on earth.[16]

We know that numerous denominational groups can look back
at their incredible growth over the last few decades and sense that
God has uniquely helped them to grow. All of this points to the
fact that the gospel is being spread throughout the world. Hundreds of years before the birth of Christ, the prophet Joel predicted such growth:

> Afterward,
>   I will pour out my Spirit on all people.
> Your sons and daughters will prophesy,
>   your old men will dream dreams,
> your young men will see visions.
> Even on my servants, both men and women,
>   I will pour out my Spirit in those days.
> I will show wonders in the heavens
>   and on the earth,
>   blood and fire and billows of smoke.
> The sun will be turned to darkness
>   and the moon to blood
>   before the coming of the great and dreadful day of the LORD.
> And everyone who calls
>   on the name of the LORD will be saved. (Joel 2:28–32)

As we look at the growth in Christianity worldwide and, sadly,
at the growth of non-Christian religions, we can have a realization
that Bible prophecy is being fulfilled.

Speaking of the last days, Daniel said, "None of the wicked will
understand, but those who are wise will understand" (Dan. 12:10).

Technology

The growth of technology is another clear sign that the end
could be near. Having been given insight about the last days,

Daniel was told, "Many will go here and there to increase knowledge" (Dan. 12:4). Today there is more knowledge than at any other time in history. Billy Graham said, "I read recently that 90 percent of all the scientists and engineers who have ever lived are alive today. Our high schools, colleges, and universities are turning out nearly 4 million graduates every year."[17] The explosion of scientific knowledge, technological advances in transportation, communications, the computer, and military hardware would have been unimaginable at the beginning of the twentieth century.

As we watch the clock of time pass from this century to the next, what will the future hold? It is estimated that by 2063 the world's crude-oil reserves will run out (based on current production rates). By 2150 it is projected that the world population will be 10,806,000,000 (nearly twice the population of today) and life expectancy will be eighty-six years.[18]

Daniel's prophecy of a great increase of knowledge is being fulfilled right before our eyes. Time/Life reports,

> We are about to enter a millennium of miracles. If a person cuts off his hand while fixing a lawn mower, doctors will be able to grow him a new one. Houses and cars will be made of materials that can fix themselves when damaged. There will be a white powdered food that is 90 percent protein and can be made to taste like almost anything.
>
> These predictions may sound bold, but in truth they're pretty conservative. Replaceable limbs? Scientists began regenerating human skin in the 1970s, and doctors who have successfully regenerated heart valves from just a few cells say the era of replaceable body parts is inevitable. As for self-repairing building materials, there's already a metal, Nitinol, that can fix its own dents with a simple application of heat. The miracle food? It's called soy isolate, and Archer Daniels Midland has been shipping it around the world since the 1980s.
>
> Computers, the electronic brains behind intelligent metals, miraculous foods and replaceable organs, are growing smarter by the minute. According to Moore's Law (propounded

by Gordon Moore, cofounder of Intel), they get twice as smart every 18 to 24 months. They are already 3,300 times smarter than when microprocessors were introduced in 1971. Paul Horn, senior vice president of research at IBM, says Moore's Law will apply for at least another 15 years. This means that when country singer LeAnn Rimes is 31, computers will be nearly 200 times more powerful than those we use today—or roughly 660,000 times more powerful than the first micro-processor.[19]

Just a few years ago many wondered how the Scripture would be fulfilled that says that the whole world will watch as two powerful preachers of the gospel are killed on the streets of Jerusalem during the tribulation (see Rev. 11:9–10). But when the Russian Sputnik satellite was sent into the sky on October 4, 1957, the world of communications radically changed. Now, over forty years later, we have numerous satellites circling the earth making it possible to have instantaneous communication. Cameras can literally be taken everywhere and link up with a satellite that can transfer the event right into your living room.

The Bible tells us that during the tribulation the associate of the antichrist will be able to force everyone to receive a mark on his right hand or on his forehead, so that no one can buy or sell unless he has the mark (Rev. 13:16–17). This is no longer difficult to imagine since most everything we buy at the supermarket is run over a scanner that gives the computer the price of the item we are purchasing. Not only that, the machine takes inventory and tells managers when to reorder stock. We do not know how the antichrist will "mark" every human being, but one can imagine possible scenarios.

Politics

The worldwide political arena is constantly changing. There is great concern over who will lead Russia next: Will he be conservative, communist, in favor of the West? Any change in the Middle East is nervously watched. Will a new leader decide to unleash a nuclear weapon on some nearby country and draw the United States into a bloodbath?

The economic frustrations of countries in the Orient and the West and in third-world countries could motivate these nations to find leadership that will do whatever it takes to get their people on stable ground, even if that means changing alliances with those they have previously supported.

For years the United Nations has done everything it can to find and destroy any ability Saddam Hussein might have to develop and hide chemical weapons or a nuclear bomb. Like the tide of the ocean, Saddam draws back for a time then rushes in, the difference being that he is unpredictable. As the NATO bombing in Yugoslavia shows, many countries in Eastern Europe remain unstable and can erupt at any moment. The U.N. continues to intervene in the hostilities of numerous nations every day. They understand that the nations of the world are armed and ready to attack or defend themselves. The United States spends hundreds of billions of dollars on armaments. There is no peace on this earth because it is full of wars and rumors of wars, nations and kingdoms at battle.

With more and more unstable countries obtaining the information, materials, and manpower to build a nuclear weapon, it is not difficult to imagine that someone will push the wrong button either on purpose or by accident. We could wake up tomorrow morning and find that we are in World War III. Jesus said, "You will hear of wars and rumors of wars, but see to it that you are not alarmed. Such things must happen, but the end is still to come. Nation will rise against nation, and kingdom against kingdom" (Matt. 24:6–7).

The emergence of the "balance of terror" (nuclear and chemical weapons and their proliferation) together with wars and rumors of wars, the development of a European confederacy of ten nations (Dan. 11; Rev. 17), the emergence of China as a world power (Dan. 11; Rev. 9), and the movement of Russia into the Middle East (Ezek. 38–39; Dan. 11) all are signs that remind us that we could be the terminal generation. I am not speaking about humans destroying the earth (that will not happen), but about the generation that is alive at the time of the rapture of the church witnessing these events and sensing the political tension around the world. Jesus said, "See to it that you are not alarmed."

Israel

Have you ever wondered why so much attention is given to the nation of Israel and why so many countries are concerned about the welfare of such a small country? If I didn't read my Bible, I would wonder the same thing. Hundreds of times Scripture reminds us of God's love for this land and people. The Bible points directly at this geographical location and the Jewish people as a sign of the soon coming of Jesus Christ.

Bible scholar John Phillips wrote,

> Many times in the past people have thought that the return of Christ was at hand. When the Christian era reached its one thousandth year, many thought that Christ must appear. When Islam swept like a raging fury across the Middle East, Africa, and Europe, it seemed that the end was at hand. When the French revolution steeped a nation in blood and then elevated a military genius by the name of Napoleon, it seemed again as though the final actors had taken the stage. In more recent times, when Mussolini tried to reconstitute the Roman empire, many thought he was the antichrist. But no matter what configuration of world events seemed to come together in times past, one vital factor was always missing. Israel had not been reborn as a nation. Now it has been. That is the difference between the shadows of the past and the substance of today. The fact that Israel is back in the land adds a new urgency to our conviction; end-time events can now take their ultimate shape.[20]

End-time Old Testament Scriptures make it clear that the Lord will return when the Jews are back in their land, Israel (Ezek. 37), and in their capital city, Jerusalem (Zech. 12). Many scholars feel that Jesus was emphasizing these two events when he gave the fig tree parable in Matthew 24:32–35 and speaking of the reoccupation of Jerusalem in Luke 21:24. The Bible predicted the regathering of the Jewish people from around the globe (Isa. 11), the reestablishment of the nation of Israel (Isa. 66), and the reclamation of the land (Isa. 35). Zechariah predicted the resurgence of the Israeli military (Zech. 12) and the world's focus on this tiny land (Zech. 12–14).

Until this century the fulfillment of these prophecies seemed impossible. The Romans had destroyed Jerusalem less than a century after Christ's ascension, and for hundreds of years the Jewish people were dispersed throughout the world. But on May 14, 1948, the independence of the nation of Israel was announced. This Jewish state was reborn almost two thousand years after its destruction. On June 7, 1967, the Jewish people once again took control of Jerusalem. Today we are witnessing an incredible phenomenon. Jewish people from throughout the world are returning to the nation of their heritage. This major prophecy is now in place, pointing to the urgency of the hour in which we live.

As we near the end of the most advanced century in the history of this earth, worldwide the signs of insecurity and threats of war are all around us. Daily we hear of famines, earthquakes, unusual weather patterns, amazing technological advances, and the growth of evil, cults, and the occult. Add to that the fact that a phenomenal revival is ushering tens of thousands of people into God's kingdom every day. Jesus said, "When these things begin to take place, stand up and lift up your heads, because your redemption is drawing near" (Luke 21:28).

Choose to Be a Witness

AS WE CONSIDER THE critical time in which we live, we should be motivated to tell as many people as possible about the gospel of Jesus Christ. We can choose to be a witness. Explaining the simple gospel to a friend is something we can all do. Most people come to Christ because someone has taken the time to talk with them and explain how they can give their life to Christ. You may feel nervous or feel that you do not have the words to properly explain the gospel. Most people feel that way. I have felt that way and still do from time to time.

Who are your neighbors? Do you have friends, relatives, peers in your workplace, and people you frequently associate with who do not know Jesus? Today, decide that you are going to witness to at least one of them.

We are not only to look up and wait for the rapture. We are to work with greater diligence because the time is short. Robert Coleman said, "Anticipation of our Lord's return is a summons to action. We must cast off anything that blocks the flow of the Holy Spirit and commit ourselves to being about the Father's business. World evangelization now is the responsibility around which our lives should be centered. Whatever our gifts, we are all needed in the witness of the Gospel."[21] We must win all we can to the King of Kings. We must push on and push through any wall of resistance to ensure that this gospel is presented to every part of the population.

Looking at today's newspaper or listening to the evening news can be discouraging. We can become overwhelmed thinking about the possible Y2K problem or the constant news of another war, famine, or epidemic. A time will come, however, when there will be peace and worldwide security. The wars will be over. The battle will have been won on this earth, and the King of Kings will rule this earth and eternity. The prophet Isaiah foretold that day.

> For to us a child is born
>   to us a son is given,
>   and the government will be on his shoulders.
> And he will be called
>   Wonderful Counselor, Mighty God,
>   Everlasting Father, Prince of Peace.
> Of the increase of his government and peace
>   there will be no end.

> He will reign on David's throne
>   and over his kingdom,
> establishing and upholding it
>   with justice and righteousness
>   from that time on and forever.
> The zeal of the LORD Almighty
>   will accomplish this (Isa. 9:6–7).

The signs are all around us. At any moment the Lord of Lords could appear in the clouds and believers from all over the world caught up to meet him. Are you watching? Are you doing all you can do to witness to those near you? Purpose in your heart today that you will begin to evangelize those whom the Holy Spirit brings to your mind.

Part Three

What You Can Do

⚊⚊ EIGHT ⚊⚊

Show and Tell

THE POLISHED MARINE GUARD seemed to be without personality as he appropriately asked me questions about why I was visiting the U.S. Embassy in Vienna, Austria. With a straight face and lips hardly moving, he instructed me to walk through the security gate. I was a little intimidated by all of the precaution that was taken to ensure the safety of the ambassador and his staff.

Ron, an official at the embassy, greeted me in the waiting area and walked me down the hallway. We walked to his office, and he sat behind his desk to keep an aura of formality. As I chatted with him, I couldn't help but notice that a large photograph of the president of the United States was on the wall behind his head. Whether Ron was working at his desk or meeting with an official from another country, those around him would be conscious of the president's portrait. Ron was somewhat cautious in what he said and how he acted in his high-security job. As an official at the embassy, he was responsible to demonstrate proper etiquette, to carefully select his words, and to represent the United States and the U.S. ambassador correctly. That day I saw Ron in a new light. He was not only my friend, but also a representative of the government of our great country. I knew that Ron would not compromise the security of the United States for anything.[1]

Similarly, we are "ambassadors of Christ" to this world. We are to represent God's kingdom well and to introduce as many as possible to the Leader we serve. In his booklet *How to Give Away Your Faith*, Paul Little says,

> Witnessing is that deep-seated conviction that the greatest favor I can do for others is to introduce them to Jesus Christ. "We, then, are ambassadors for Christ." This is the figure the New Testament uses to describe our role as witnesses. We are God's representatives, appointed to be his messengers. God actually makes his appeal to the world through us Christians. Imagine being an ambassador for the foreign policy of the kingdom of heaven! It's a tremendous appointment, when you think through its implications.[2]

THE BIBLE TELLS US,

> Therefore, if anyone is in Christ, he is a new creation; the old has gone, the new has come! All this is from God, who reconciled us to himself through Christ and gave us the ministry of reconciliation: that God was reconciling the world to himself in Christ, not counting men's sins against them. And he has committed to us the message of reconciliation. We are therefore Christ's ambassadors, as though God were making his appeal through us. (2 Cor. 5:17–20)

To be a successful ambassador for Christ, it is necessary to have a biblical worldview and to be sensitive to where unbelievers are in their thinking. We represent the King of Kings, and we must know the principles of his kingdom and endeavor to motivate people to become part of it.

Evangelism Principles

People are lost without Jesus Christ.

When people are not born again, they are spiritually lost and blinded to the truth found in Jesus Christ. They may be committed religious persons, sold on their particular doctrine, or may seem to have some truth because they are Buddhist, Hindu, Islamic, Mormon, or New-Agers. But they do not know the truth that will get them to heaven. "There is one God and one media-tor between God and men, the man Christ Jesus" (1 Tim. 2:5). Without Christ, people are on their way to an eternal hell.

The whole world is accountable to God (Rom. 3:19). One is not justified by doing certain acts or "keeping the law" (Rom. 3:20). Those outside of Christ are dead in their sins and are a part of the dominion of darkness (Eph. 2:1–3; Col. 1:13). The god of this world has blinded the minds of those who do not know Jesus Christ (2 Cor. 4:4). But, "whoever believes in him shall not perish but have eternal life" (John 3:16). Jesus said, "If you do not believe that I am the one I claim to be, you will indeed die in your sins" (John 8:24).

This fact can be a tremendous motivation for us as we talk to our friends and relatives about Christ. We do not want to see any-one go to hell. If people really believed that their friends or rela-tives were going to hell, with its endless horrors, they would do anything they could to win them to the Lord. The Bible tells us, "Salvation is found in no one else, for there is no other name under heaven given to men by which we must be saved" (Acts 4:12).

God desires everyone to be saved.

A critical theme runs through the entire Bible: God loves all people and wants to bring them to himself. The Scripture tells us that "God our Savior . . . *wants all men to be saved* and to come to the knowledge of the truth" (1 Tim. 2:3–5, italics added). "For *God so loved the world* that he gave his one and only Son, that *whoever believes in him* shall not perish but have eternal life" (John 3:16, italics added). "Go into *all the world* and preach the good news to all creation" (Mark 16:15, italics added).

Looking a little deeper, there are three specific places in the Bible where this thought stands out:

First, in Genesis 12:1–3 God informed Abraham that all *peoples* of the earth would be blessed through him. The original word used in the Old Testament is *mishepachah*, which refers to the family or clan and is used in Genesis 10:5 to speak of the families of nations.

Later in the New Testament, Paul explained that the content of this blessing was the good news of salvation by faith (Gal. 3:8).

Second, in what is called the Great Commission, Jesus said that we are to make disciples of the *ethne,* which is translated as "nations" (Matt. 28:19). This word is used primarily in the sense of *people* and is found sixty-four times in the New Testament in this general sense. When combined with *panta* ("all") it refers to all nations. The idea found in *ethnos* is that of a group that is bound by the same manners, customs, and other distinctive features. It does not convey the idea of a nation in the geopolitical sense but rather in the ethnolinguistic sense.

Third, we see in Revelation 5:9 and 7:9 that around the throne of God there are people from every tribe, language, people, and nation *(ethne).* It is God's desire to reconcile to himself people from every ethnic group in the world. Only when the church of Jesus Christ goes into all the world (every ethnic group) will the end come (see Matt. 24:14). Many think we are very close.

Both we and the Holy Spirit have roles to play in reaching others.

Concerning his death, burial, and resurrection, Jesus said, "It is for your good that I am going away. Unless I go away, the Counselor will not come to you; but if I go, I will send him to you. When he comes, he will convict the world of guilt in regard to sin and righteousness and judgment" (John 16:7–8).

Although God could use the Holy Spirit alone to win people to himself, he chooses to use us too. The Holy Spirit speaks to people's hearts before we speak to them about Christ, and he also reminds people of what we have said after we have talked with them. He is thoroughly involved in the process. Theologian Donald Stamps explains,

> The Spirit's ministry of convicting operates in three areas. (a) Sin. The Holy Spirit will expose sin and unbelief in order to awaken a consciousness of guilt and need for forgiveness.

Conviction also makes clear the fearful results if the guilty persist in their wrongdoing. After conviction, a choice must be made. This will often lead to true repentance and a turning to Jesus as Lord and Savior (Ac. 2:37–38). (b) Righteousness. The Spirit convinces people that Jesus is the righteous Son of God, resurrected, vindicated and now the Lord of all. He makes them aware of God's standard of righteousness in Christ, shows them what sin is and gives them power to overcome the world (Ac. 3:12–16; 7:51–60; 17:31; 1 Pe. 3:18). (c) Judgment. The Spirit convinces people of Satan's defeat at the cross (12:31; 16:11), God's present judgment of the world (Ro. 1:18–32) and the future judgment of the entire human race (Mt. 16:27; Ac. 17:31; 24:25; Ro. 14:10; 1 Co. 6:2; 2 Co. 5:10; Jude 14).[3]

A biblical example of the Holy Spirit and a person working together toward the conversion of someone is when Jesus' disciple Philip witnessed to an Ethiopian official. The Bible tells us:

> On his way [Philip] met an Ethiopian eunuch, an important official in charge of all the treasury of Candace, queen of the Ethiopians. This man had gone to Jerusalem to worship, and on his way home was sitting in his chariot reading the book of Isaiah the prophet. The Spirit told Philip, "Go to that chariot and stay near it."
>
> Then Philip ran up to the chariot and heard the man reading Isaiah the prophet. "Do you understand what you are reading?" Philip asked.
>
> "How can I," he said, "unless someone explains it to me?" So he invited Philip to come up and sit with him.
>
> The eunuch was reading this passage of Scripture:
>
> > "He was led like a sheep to the slaughter,
> >   and as a lamb before the shearer is silent,
> >   so he did not open his mouth.
> > In his humiliation he was deprived of justice.
> >   Who can speak of his descendants?
> >   For his life was taken from the earth."

The eunuch asked Philip, "Tell me, please, who is the prophet talking about, himself or someone else?" Then Philip began with that very passage of Scripture and told him the good news about Jesus.

As they traveled along the road, they came to some water and the eunuch said, "Look, here is water. Why shouldn't I be baptized?" (Acts 8:27–36)

In this remarkable conversion story, the Ethiopian needed Philip to tell him what the Spirit drew his attention to (Acts 8). The Holy Spirit is involved in a person's conversion and in our ability to communicate the gospel to that person much more than we realize. His work is often very complex. George Barna explains that there are different levels on which the effectiveness of evangelistic efforts must be examined.

The first level is the *supernatural:* no matter how accomplished we are in evangelism, it is not our efforts but those of the Holy Spirit which cause a person to accept Christ. The Spirit's role in the evangelistic process may be somewhat mysterious to us, but we know for sure that it is the Spirit's job and ability to bring a seeking person to true faith in Christ.

The second level relates to our *evangelistic competence*. While it is the Spirit who causes a person to follow Christ, God works through people to influence the decisions of non-believers. Thus, we may examine the nature of the evangelistic interactions Christians have with non-believers to understand how well-equipped we are for the task, and how well we handle the opportunities we experience.

The third level has to do with *measurement*. Only God truly knows if a person is a Christian. We use measurement tools such as surveys to gain an approximation of evangelistic impact, but we will never have perfect information—not an exact understanding of how well or how poorly we are performing our duties.[4]

Every Christian is called to be a witness.

In his last statement to his disciples before he left this earth, Jesus said, "'You will receive power when the Holy Spirit comes on you; and you will be my witnesses" (Acts 1:8). Everyone is to be a witness for Christ, and everyone needs the supernatural ability given by the Holy Spirit. Not everyone is an evangelist, but everyone should be evangelizing.

Some encouraging indicators point to the idea that people are in fact verbally witnessing to others. In his book *Evangelism That Works,* Barna lists several.

- Interpersonal evangelism is alive and evident. During the past year, more than 60 million adults (one-third of the adult population) claim to have shared their religious beliefs with someone they felt had different religious beliefs in the hope that the recipient might accept Jesus Christ as personal Savior.
- The people who share their faith with nonbelievers do so often. On average, lay evangelists share with one person every month. Projected through the course of a year, this suggests that nearly three-quarters of a billion evangelistic conversations take place each year in America.

To get the complete picture, however, you must add to this the exposure of TV viewers to evangelistic pitches made by people such as Billy Graham, Charles Stanley, Pat Robertson and others. Invitations to accept Christ that are heard through Christian radio programming; the millions of pieces of evangelistic literature that are distributed; Christian books that are written for the purpose of leading a person to accept Christ as personal Savior; Christian songs that are played on the airwaves and Christian videos that are watched on TV; and the numerous evangelistic sermons and invitations at church services and other events.

The bottom line is that more than one billion evangelistic invitations are shared every year in America. If it were possible to accurately count the number of evangelistic exposures made through this vast array of communication methods, it likely would exceed 3 billion in the United States.

- Although it is true that nearly half of all adults indicate they become annoyed when someone tries to share religious beliefs with them, we also have discovered that when those same annoyed individuals have an evangelistic conversation through the witness of a family member, close friend or trusted associate, they are not annoyed. Depending upon the state of mind or point of spiritual quest of the nonbeliever, the person may even express gratitude for the interest shown in them.
- Much of evangelism fails to result in conversions. The task of the Christian, however, is to be faithful in sharing the gospel. It is the job of the Holy Spirit to complete the process by leading the nonbeliever to decide to follow Christ. Success in evangelism is obedience to the call to evangelize, not the number of conversions in which a person plays a part.
- Billy Graham has been one of the great evangelists in world history. God has used him mightily throughout the world for [more than] four decades. To suggest, however, that the era of evangelism will close with his retirement is like suggesting that no more churches would be planted after the death of the apostle Paul. God does not rely upon one single person.

Today, more than 3,000 people serve as itinerant evangelists, much as Dr. Graham has served. They use a variety of methods to bring the gospel to the people, ranging from massive crusades to one-on-one conversations, and are living proof that evangelism will continue well into the next century.

- Every year, approximately 1 million people receive some kind of evangelism training. In most cases, this consists of classes or other preparation provided by their churches. In other situations, this equipping occurs in classes at schools and seminaries, in seminars and conferences on evangelistic activity, in personal mentoring and in training offered by parachurch ministries such as Evangelism Explosion, Campus Crusade for Christ and the Billy Graham Evangelistic Association. Overall, among the 60 million adults who shared their faith with non-Christians last year, almost half of them (47 percent) have had some form of evangelism training during their lifetimes.5

Ken Hutchenson, former professional football star and now pastor of a thriving church in Seattle, Washington, said,

> If you're going to do anything without the Holy Spirit, don't do anything at all. Did you understand that statement? If you're going to do something without the Holy Spirit, the easiest thing to do without Him is nothing at all. That's the best and the finest thing to do without Him. Do nothing and you won't get into trouble. Do nothing and you won't be a stumbling block to God's people and a detriment to God's work in the world. That's the one thing God in His grace and kindness allows us to do to please Him apart from His Holy Spirit. Nothing! (And really it doesn't please Him at all, because He wants us to use our gifts to bless and serve Christ's body, the church.)
>
> The point is, do nothing . . . until you are filled with the Holy Spirit. And then—hang on to your hat! He'll have you doing things beyond what you ever imagined.6

God initiates salvation and draws people to Christ.

The Father draws people to Jesus through the Holy Spirit. Jesus said, "No one can come to me unless the Father who sent me draws him" (John 6:44). All three members of the godhead are involved in a person's salvation experience. God's work of drawing involves all people. Jesus said, "I . . . will draw all men to myself" (John 12:32), but God's drawing can be resisted. People can choose to resist the attempts of God and others to bring them to Christ. Knowing that God is constantly drawing people to his Son gives us tremendous comfort. He takes the initiative and continually works on people's hearts.

There is a definite connection between signs and wonders and people's response to Christ.

Missiologist Peter Wagner says, "Worldwide, Pentecostal churches grow when the Holy Spirit is free to manifest His miracle power through believers."[7] An example of explosive church growth is China. Wagner believes such rapid growth is a result of God's immediate supernatural work of healing, casting out of demons, and performing miracles.[8] The emphasis on spiritual gifts has also led to what J. I. Packer calls "an unprecedented willingness to experiment with new structure and liturgical forms for church life, so as to make room for the full use of all gifts for the benefit of the whole congregation."[9]

Throughout the book of Acts we see signs and wonders working together with evangelism. Here are some examples:

Signs and Wonders	*Evangelism/Church Growth*
2:1–4 People were filled with the Holy Spirit and spoke in tongues	**2:41–43** About three thousand were added to their number
3:1–8 Crippled man was healed	**3:10; 4:3–4** "They were filled with wonder"; the number of men grew to about five thousand
5:1–13 Ananias and Sapphira lied to the Holy Spirit and died as a result	**5:14–15** "More and more . . . believed"
6:1–8 "Stephen . . . did great wonders and miraculous signs"	**6:7** "The number of disciples . . . increased rapidly"

Signs and Wonders

8:6–7
"Crowds heard Philip and saw the miraculous signs he did"

9:17–19
Saul was healed and filled with the Holy Spirit

9:32–34
Paralytic was healed

9:36–41
Tabitha was raised from the dead

11:15
"The Holy Spirit came on them as ... at the beginning"

12:20–23
Herod was struck down (was eaten by worms and died)

13:8–11
Elymas the sorcerer was made blind

14:3
Paul and Barnabas were enabled to do "miraculous signs and wonders"

16:25–26
Prison was opened by earthquake for Paul and Silas

19:11
"God did extraordinary miracles through Paul"

Evangelism/Church Growth

8:12
"They believed Philip as he preached the Good News"

9:31
The church grew in numbers

9:35
All those who saw him turned to the Lord

9:42
"Many people believed"

11:21
"A great number ... believed"

12:24
"Word of God continued to increase and spread"

13:12
"When the proconsul saw ... he believed"

14:21–23
"Won a large number"

16:31–34
Jailer and family believed

19:20
"The word of the Lord spread widely and grew in power"

Signs and wonders are part of God's plan for reaching the world for Christ. Nowhere does Scripture suggest that signs were restricted to the first-century church. The same spiritual gifts we read about in the New Testament can be part of our lives today. Paul said to the Corinthian church, "You do not lack any spiritual gift as you eagerly wait for our Lord Jesus Christ to be revealed" (1 Cor. 1:7). There is no question that preaching the gospel of the kingdom and "bringing in the kingdom" by the demonstration of God's power through signs and wonders catches the attention of unbelievers and builds the faith of believers.[10]

Confrontive witness is the most effective evangelism.

Recently I saw a TCI television ad that said, "Our goal is to treat every customer as if they were our only customer." That saying could be applied to evangelism. We should endeavor to win each person as if he or she were the last person to be reached.

Confrontive evangelism happens between neighbors, peers, or acquaintances. In this type of witnessing, we pray about witnessing to a certain person and plan a time to do it. I call this making a "divine appointment." We share the gospel with the individual, and we may ask whether he or she would like to make a commitment to Jesus Christ. This approach often has good results.

The setting of the encounter might be the unbeliever's home, a sporting activity, concert, public place, or even an airplane or bus. Just about anyplace you can think of can be used to confront others with the gospel.

The longer you're saved, the fewer unsaved acquaintances you have, yet the greatest form of evangelism is friend to friend evangelism.

Most Christians can say they have few, if any, non-Christian friends. We also know that the longer we are Christians, the less we think like non-Christians. In *The Purpose Driven Church,* pastor and author Rick Warren explains numerous strategies and programs he uses to attract the non-Christian to the church where he serves. He also reminds his congregation, "The longer you are a believer, the less you think like an unbeliever."[11] His point in saying this is that to reach unbelievers, we must find ways to befriend them, identify with them without compromise, and help them in the areas where they have pain in their lives. George Barna is of the same opinion. He feels we need to ensure that we have "evangelistic competence." "While it is the Spirit who causes a person to follow Christ, God works through people to influence the decisions of non-believers. Thus, we may examine the nature of the evangelistic interactions Christians have with non-believers to understand how well-equipped we are for the task, and how well we handle the opportunities we experience."[12] God uses many ways to draw people to Christ. Barna researched this subject and asked, What approaches lead people to Christ? This is the breakdown for how people come to Christ:

44% personal/family witnessing
13% church sermon
5% evangelistic event/crusade
5% personal evangelism by a clergyman
5% physical healing
4% Sunday school class
4% youth camp/event
4% death of relative or friend
16% other means[13]

By far the most successful way to reach people for Christ is through friendship or family relationship.

One of the great dangers for a church is when they exclusively focus on their own needs and lose concern for reaching the community and world outside their walls. Peter Wagner has called this "koinonitis." *Koinonia* is a scriptural word for fellowship, and Christian fellowship is a wonderful benefit of being a Christian; however, too much Christian fellowship causes us to be "ingrown."

Koinonitis occurs when church members, having worked to build strong, meaningful, interpersonal relationships with each other, begin behaving exclusively rather than inclusively. Adopting an us vs. them mentality, where church members have no desire to leave their secure protected comfort zones to comfort the world of church visitors and new believers. Instead of existing to spread the gospel, such a church exists only for itself and its members.[14]

Paul Little says,

Genuine Christians want to live holy lives. But it is Satan who tries to convince us that if we clan together and avoid all unnecessary contact with non-Christians, we will not be contaminated by the world around us. By his devilish logic he has persuaded us that true spirituality is to separate ourselves totally from the world around us. Some Christians have told me with evident pride that no non-Christian has ever been inside their homes. With an air of "spirituality," they have boasted that they have no non-Christian friends. No wonder they have never had the joy of introducing someone to the Savior![15]

The gospel message has an inherent power.

Whenever the gospel is shared, God honors it. Not only is the entire godhead involved in a person's salvation experience, but the gospel message itself has incredible power. We can be assured that when we share the gospel with someone, the Holy Spirit will use this truth to speak to his or her heart. The apostle Paul said, "I am not ashamed of the gospel, because it is the power of God for the salvation of everyone who believes" (Rom. 1:16).

What an assurance we can have when we are actively endeavoring to be a witness for Christ. God has literally done everything he can to demonstrate his wonderful love to all people, and he has given us everything we need to reach others for Jesus.

America's Final Call?

"AMERICA IS AT A TURNING POINT IN ITS HISTORY," George Barna informs us in his book *The Second Coming of the Church:*

The decisions we make in the next few years regarding who we are and the values we stand for will seal the moral and spiritual fate of America for decades to come. The decadence and darkness of our nation are more profound than since the founding of this nation more than two centuries ago. The only power that can cleanse and restore this nation is the power of Christ. And the primary way in which that power is manifested is by Christ's followers serving God and humanity by being the Church—that is, the true representative of Jesus Christ.

This is our time of testing. We must prove that we are what we claim to be, or we will certainly lose the platform to influence the world for Christ. That privileged position is already slipping from our grasp. Given the moral and spiritual demise of our culture, maintaining that position is not an insignificant challenge. And the sad truth is that the Christian church, as we now know it, is not geared up to meet that challenge.

Our situation is not hopeless, but it is urgent. Time is of the essence. Godly, strategic leadership, dedicated to the fulfillment of God's vision for America and His church, is demanded.[16]

The church of Jesus Christ is not a building, nor is it a particular denomination. It is made up of people who have made Jesus Christ their Lord and Savior and have accepted the atoning sacrifice he made on the cross. God does not favor the church in America over the church in any other country. Christian people who live in Iran, Albania, Romania, Cuba, Saudi Arabia, India, Mexico, and throughout the whole world (including every believer who has ever lived) are part of his marvelous church. Wherever the people of God are, there is a church.

Nowhere does Jesus command the unsaved to go to church. Rather, he commands the church to go to the unsaved. In Matthew he tells us to "go and make disciples" (Matt. 28:19). In Mark he instructs us to "go into all the world" (Mark 16:15). In Luke he informs his disciples that "this is what is written:...

Repentance and forgiveness of sins will be preached in [Jesus']
name to all nations" (Luke 24:46–47). And in Acts he says, "You
will be my witnesses . . . to the ends of the earth" (Acts 1:8). Over
and over, God instructs the church to "go," while he continually
invites those without Christ to "come."

Paul tells us that God's people comprise "God's household,
which is the church of the living God, the pillar and foundation of
the truth" (1 Tim. 3:15). Even though we believe in a strong educational system and we support and pray for our government, it is
the church that is to be the real communicator of truth. What is
the truth? The Bible tells us that the Holy Spirit, whom God gives
to every Christian, is our Counselor and is "the Spirit of truth"
(John 14:17). The truth is found in knowing Jesus Christ, "the way,
the truth, and the life," who promised that "the Counselor, the
Holy Spirit, whom the Father will send in my name, will teach you
all things and will remind you of everything I have said to you"
(John 14:26). The church introduces reality into a very confused
and lost world. It is the conscience of society and the pillar that
holds the truth of Jesus Christ up to a world that constantly dis-
obeys and compromises God's truth.

The church is the most powerful institution on earth, and God
working through the church can change laws, policies, opinions,
standards, and even societies within governments. This is why we
need to be deeply concerned about the church of America. While
revival is breaking out in many parts of the world, much of the
church in our nation is at a standstill. We must do all we can to
revive America's church, or we may lose many blessings that our
gracious Lord has bestowed on this nation.

James Dobson of Focus on the Family says,

> Many laymen may not know that the institution of the
> church is undergoing serious difficulty at this time. Many
> local churches are barely surviving with approximately
> 3,000–4,000 of them closing their doors every year. Pollster
> George Barna compared the church to the Titanic when he
> said, "It is large, elegant, and sinking fast."

Attendance at weekly religious activities in the United States has continued to slip to 49 percent in 1991 and to 37 percent today. Furthermore, 80 percent of the church growth results from transfers of memberships. In other words, relatively few new commitments to Christ appear to be occurring. These statistics tell us that evangelism is largely stagnant, and yet, 96 percent of adults say they still believe in God. Something is wrong with this picture. Obviously, a minority of Americans are dabbling in religious expression that has no substance.

This is an alarming situation. As the Christian church in North America continues to decline and its influence weakens, the nation is falling further into immorality and wickedness. Superstition attracts millions to astrology, psychic readers and ESP. Others are concocting home-made theologies based on everything from New Age nonsense to Eastern mysticism, in a search for meaning and security. A large proportion of today's younger generation has no memory of the gospel of Jesus Christ and the teachings of Scripture. This is what happens in a culture when the church loses its effectiveness and zeal. We must do everything we can to support this basic institution which God has ordained and blessed.[17]

You can make a difference.

Just as one at a time people make choices to give their lives to Christ, so too we can choose to be the witness that God desires us to be. We in the church can choose to live a life that will make people want the Lord we serve.

Professional golfer Bobby Clampett was on the PGA Tour from 1980 to 1995 and is now a sportscaster with CBS Sports. His best finish came in 1982 when he won the Southern Open in Columbus, Georgia. Bobby is a committed Christian who founded Players Outreach Ministries. When asked how he came to his Christian faith, he said,

People come to Christ in different ways. For some it's a slow process. There are key players God put in my path.

The most significant impact occurred when I met my wife. She had been brought up in the church and made a commitment to Christ when she was 17. We met my third year of the PGA. I was still hanging on to the preconceived church beliefs that I had picked up in the Christian Science church and the Mormon church. We enjoyed talking about spiritual issues, and both of us were seekers of truth.

There were many questions that couldn't be answered by the Christian Scientists or Mormons. I knew there was objective truth out there, but I didn't want to join a church and commit intellectual suicide. My wife played a big part in the process, and so did other Christians on the tour. I was moving toward the belief that the Bible was the inspired Word of God and that Jesus is who He claimed to be. I began to realize I had never made a decision to trust Him for my salvation and allow Him to change me and be at the forefront of my life. I did that in July 1984. I was very self-centered before then.

God has changed me. It was the one decision that has most profoundly impacted my life.

Bobby is not only enjoying his new life in Christ, but he is actively sharing his faith with others. When asked about the spiritual climate in the PGA and whether he believes there is a spiritual hunger among professional golfers he said:

No question about it. The PGA Tour Bible study began in 1966 with five players. The study has grown tremendously. There are 250 or so players on the tour, and 70 have made a public confession of Christ.

It's just amazing to watch the power of God at work in the lives of people. I'm excited to see people deepen their walk with God and seek truth. We're blessed on the PGA Tour with people who are diligently seeking God. They are not seeking some spiritual thing to hold onto; they're looking for truth. Players are seeking answers to life's deeper questions. I think specifically in my age group—I'm 38—there seems to be a real awakening. I believe we are in a time of spiritual awakening.[18]

Early in Bobby Clampett's Christian experience he realized that he could choose to evangelize people one at a time. Like Bobby, you can choose to be a witness. Today you can talk to a family member, a friend, or even a stranger about the greatest truth anyone can ever know.

⊷ Nine ⊶

Improving the Odds

A SPEAKER TOLD THE story about how Abraham Lincoln visited a slave auction one day and was appalled by the sights and sounds of buying and selling human beings. Lincoln's heart was particularly drawn to a young woman on the block who looked hardened by the years of abuse she had already endured. She stared with contempt and hatred at everyone around her. The humiliation of being auctioned off to the highest bidder was so dehumanizing she could barely endure it.

The auctioneer began the bidding, and Lincoln offered a bid. As others shouted their bids, Lincoln counter-bid until he won. He went forward and handed the auctioneer the money and took ownership of the young woman. She stared at him with contempt and asked him what he was going to do with her. He said, "I'm going to set you free."

"Free?" she asked. "Free for what?"

"Just free," Lincoln answered.

"Completely free? Free to do whatever I want to do?" she challenged him.

"Yes," he said. "Free to do whatever you want to do."

"Free to say whatever I want to say?"

"Yes, free to say whatever you want to say."

"Free to go wherever I want to go?" she added with skepticism.

Lincoln answered, "You are free to go anywhere you want to go."

"Then I'm going with you!" she said with a smile.[1]

This young woman knew that the person who purchased her was different from anyone who had previously owned her. She believed she was safe with this man called Lincoln and knew that she had better stay with someone she could trust.

This story reminds me of the time many followers turned away from Jesus and he asked the Twelve, "You do not want to leave too, do you?" (John 6:67). Simon Peter answered him, "Lord to whom shall we go? You have the words of eternal life. We believe and know that you are the Holy One of God" (John 6:68–69).

Peter understood that he had found the answer to life. He knew that outside of Christ his existence was empty and meaningless. Where could he go to find the truth he had heard Jesus communicate? What could he do to obtain the kind of peace he felt when he was with this man? Who could do the kinds of miracles Jesus performed? And who could ever love him in the way that Peter sensed Jesus loved him? Deep inside, Peter was certain that Jesus was the "Holy One of God" (the Christ), and he was determined to stay as close to him as he could.

Author and founder of Evangelism Explosion, D. James Kennedy, writes, "A disciple is a functional, maturing, reproducing follower of Jesus Christ."[2] Disciples of Jesus are loyal to him. Because of their living relationship with him, they understand that they have personally met the one who is "the way, and the truth and the life" (John 14:6). They have made the choice to follow him.

We are constantly making choices. Throughout the Bible we see the results of good and bad choices. Adam and Eve made a wrong choice when they decided to disobey God's instructions. They broke his law and passed on the results of the rebellion to their children and to you and to me. All of us are capable of disobedience, rebellion, and sin. David said, "Surely I was sinful at birth, sinful from the time my mother conceived me" (Ps. 51:5). We can choose to live a life of sin, or we can choose to make Jesus the Lord of our life. Disciples understand that their loyalties are with Jesus. They have chosen to deny themselves and be loyal to their Savior.

William Barclay says,

Peter's loyalty was based on a personal relationship to Jesus Christ. There were many things he did not understand; he was just as bewildered and puzzled as anyone else. But there was something about Jesus for which he would willingly die. In the last analysis Christianity is not a philosophy which we accept, nor a theory to which we give allegiance. It is a personal response to Jesus Christ. It is the allegiance and the love which a man gives because his heart will not allow him to do anything else.[3]

Spiritual Defection

BUT WHAT ABOUT THOSE WHO DEFECT? Scripture tells us that "many of his disciples turned back and no longer followed him" (John 6:66). Why do people walk away from Christ? People drift away for many reasons.

Some people decide that they are not willing to completely obey the Lord. After they hear about Christ, they quickly decide they would like to be Christian. After contemplation about living for Jesus, however, they decide they really do not want to give up their former lifestyle and live completely for him. When they realize there is a "cross" to carry, they decide to walk away. Bill Bright of Campus Crusade says, "Tragically, many Christians today are not true disciples of our Lord Jesus Christ. Instead, they are content to 'play church' while living a materialistic and selfish lifestyle. Yet many others have demonstrated sacrificial love for God and for building His kingdom."[4]

Other people do not like the idea of suffering for Jesus. They are takers and not givers, and their motivation for coming to Christ is to get something. They misunderstand that they could never outgive God—with all of his mercy, kindness, and goodness. They soon realize that there is a price for discipleship and a cross to carry. It is hard for some to commit when they discover they must die to themselves.

Some Christians deteriorate slowly. If we are not careful, the trials of life can wear us down and take away the excitement of our faith. Life can be cruel, and our hopes and dreams can fade if we don't keep our focus on the Lord. We can become distracted, complacent, and apathetic to the things of God, and we deteriorate.

There is a story about an artist who was painting the Last Supper. It was to be a great work, and he worked hard on it for many years. As a model for the face of Christ, he used a young man with a face of transcendent loveliness and purity. Bit by bit the picture was filled in, and one after another the disciples were painted. The day came when he needed a model for Judas, whose face he had left to the last. He went out and searched in the lowest haunts of the city and in the dens of vice. At last he found a man with a face so depraved and vicious that the artist thought he would meet his requirement for Judas. When the artist finished the painting, the man said, "You painted me before." "Surely not," said the artist. "O yes," said the man, "I sat for your Christ." The years had brought terrible deterioration.[5] If we don't keep our focus on the Lord and permit the Holy Spirit to keep our hearts right with God, we can become disillusioned and even bitter.

Many people have heard the gospel as children or perhaps have even grown up in a home where church attendance was part of their lives, but for one reason or another they began to question their faith and let life's battles distort what little Christianity they understood. The trials of life can wear nominal Christians down so that they identify more with the world around them than with the Lord they grew up hearing about.

Across the nation on any given Sunday multitudes of people respond to altar calls, but the majority do not stay committed. In his book *Bride of Heaven, Pride of Hell*, author Ray Comfort writes,

> The Bible tells us that Judas led a "multitude" to Jesus. His motive, however, wasn't to bring them to the Savior for salvation. Modern evangelism is also bringing "multitudes" to Jesus. Our motive may be different from the motive of Judas, but the end result is the same. Just as the multitudes that came to Christ under the direction of Judas fell back from the Son of God, statistics show that up to 90% of those coming to Christ under the methods of modern evangelism fall away from the faith.[6]

Spiritual Multiplication

WHAT IS THE ANSWER? How can we improve the odds of keeping those who have made a confession of faith in Christ and have committed their lives to him? I am in agreement with Bill Bright:

> There is no question in my mind that the prayers and witness of godly, Spirit-filled men and women can reverse the tide of evil that is threatening to destroy all that we hold dear and sacred in our Judeo-Christian faith. The key to changing the world is spiritual multiplication—*winning and training men and women who in turn win and train others who go on to win and train still others, spiritual generation after spiritual generation.* That is the strategy the church used in the first centuries to reach the world with God's message.[7]

SIMILARLY, D. JAMES KENNEDY FEELS THAT

> those who are satisfied with merely proclaiming the Gospel and receiving professions are like immoral seducers. The seducer is satisfied merely to exploit and then tell of his exploits rather than entering into a meaningful marriage commitment. Do not judge the effectiveness of your evangelism and discipleship by what you see in the person you have evangelized. Measure your effectiveness by your spiritual grandchildren. If those you evangelize and disciple produce good disciples who can disciple others, then you have done your job well.[8]

We must not only win people to Christ, but we must give them time while we disciple them in the ways of the Christian faith and train them to be soul winners. Charlie Wanagit of Thailand has led more than 1,500 people to Christ in the past four years. When Bill Bright was visiting him, Charlie introduced Bill to one of his disciples, who introduced Bill to one of his disciples, and so it went down a line of twelve men and women. The last disciple in the chain had been a Christian for only six months and had already introduced twelve people to Christ![9] One-on-one discipleship in the body of Christ is the most effective key for assimilating people into lifetime commitment. In fact, it is the most effective form of evangelism.

Imagine that you had the tremendous opportunity to preach and see 1,000 people a day come to Christ because of your evangelistic efforts. With today's population it would take you 15,000 years to win the world! What if you were able to preach to 100,000 people a day and saw 4000 (4 percent) respond to your messages? Not only would you become world famous, but you would see 1,460,000 people come to Christ each year. In sixteen years 23,360,000 people would have become Christians because of your evangelistic gift. If, however, you would reach one person and take six months to disciple that person, then in the next six months both you and your disciple would win another person and take six months to train that person, then in the following six months the four of you win one person and take six months to train that person, and this pattern went on for sixteen years, you and your disciples would have won 4 billion.

Spiritual multiplication is the act of purposefully discipling new Christians so that they, in turn, will evangelize and disciple others, spiritual generation after spiritual generation.[10]

Spiritual Purpose

IN HIS BEST-SELLING BOOK, *The Purpose-Driven Church®*, Rick Warren explains five essential tasks that churches should be involved in. I believe these are necessary keys of discipleship.[11] As Christians we not only should feel the urgency to win people to Christ, but we also should understand that it is critical to follow through and ensure that they become true disciples, grounded in the faith and reproducing others in Christianity. Warren explains that in discipling people we should help them understand and live in the following five purposes.

1. Love the Lord with all your heart.

The word that Warren uses to describe this purpose is *worship*. He explains that

> the church exists to worship God. How do we love God with all our heart? By worshiping him! It doesn't matter if we're by ourselves, with a small group, or with 100,000 people. When we express our love to God, we're worshiping.
>
> The Bible says, "Worship the Lord your God, and serve him only" (Matt. 4:10). Notice that worship comes before service. Worshiping God is the church's first purpose. Sometimes we get so busy working for God, we don't have time to express our love for him through worship.[12]

Our life should demonstrate a daily life of worship. We often persuade new converts to get involved in some church activity, to help in some area, or to attend church numerous times a week to stabilize them in their new commitment. These activities are important, but teaching new converts to be worshipers of God is more important than any activity. A. W. Tozer said, "We're here to be worshipers first and workers only second. We take a convert and immediately make a worker out of him. God never meant it to be so. God meant that a convert should learn to be a worshiper, and after that he can learn to be a worker.... The work done by a worshiper will have eternity in it."[13] Living a life of thankfulness, gratitude, and worship toward our heavenly Father brings a stability and confidence to one's faith that little else can duplicate.

2. Love your neighbor as yourself.

The word Warren uses to describe this purpose is *ministry*.

> The church exists to minister to people. Ministry is demonstrating God's love to others by meeting their needs and healing their hurts in the name of Jesus. Each time you reach out in love to others you are ministering to them. The church should minister to all kinds of needs: spiritual, emotional, relational, and physical. Jesus said that even a cup of

cold water given in his name was considered as ministry and would not go unrewarded. The church is to "equip the saints for the work of ministry" (Eph. 4:12 NRSV).

Unfortunately, very little actual ministry takes place in many churches. Instead, much of the time is taken up by meetings. Faithfulness is often defined in terms of attendance rather than service, and members just sit, soak, and sour.[14]

There is significant evidence that people and churches that are involved in what is called "need-orientated evangelism" have tremendous results. These evangelistic efforts focus on the questions and needs of non-Christians. This concept communicates that every Christian is responsible to use his or her own specific gift in fulfilling the Great Commission. Leaders of growing churches know who has the gift of evangelism, and these leaders are effective in directing them in need-oriented outreach.[15]

An example of need-orientated evangelism is divorce recovery programs, which often are facilitated by people who have gone through the tragedy of divorce and have experienced the healing and forgiveness of Christ. Another program I recently heard about is for women who have had an abortion. The group was formed to deal with the tremendous guilt, shame, and suffering they experience. This group meets in a private home, and the leader encourages the members to discuss their emotional pain and helps them understand that they can have complete forgiveness in Jesus Christ. Another church began a small group for those who suffer from HIV or AIDS. I will never forget hearing of a woman who attended this group, whose husband had the HIV virus. He was a state government official and had told his wife that if anyone found out he had the virus from homosexual contact, he would kill himself. His wife said that she could not find any other support groups in the community that helped HIV/AIDS victims or their relatives. As a result, she began attending the church and grew in her faith. In another church, a program was started for alcoholics and substance abusers. It is called Taste of New Wine. Each Monday a born-again, ex-alcoholic leads the group discussion and explains that Jesus—the true Higher Power—will help them make it without drugs or alcohol. For years the program has experienced tremendous success because, besides overcoming these addictions, most of the attendees become committed Christians and begin ministering to others with addictive behaviors.

Whatever type of human suffering there is, the church can develop ministry programs for the people involved. Let the Holy Spirit give you creative ideas about how to minister to people in need. I believe that people are more open to the gospel during times of need than perhaps any other time. Oswald Chambers said, "I will make the place of my feet glorious—among the poor, the devil-possessed, the mean, the decrepit, the selfish, the sinful, the misunderstood—that is where Jesus went, and that is exactly where he will take you if you are his disciple."[16]

3. Go and make disciples.

Warren calls this purpose *evangelism*. He explains,

> The church exists to communicate God's Word. We are ambassadors for Christ, and our mission is to evangelize the world. The word *go* in the Great Commission is a present participle in the Greek text. It should mean *"as you are going."* It is every Christian's responsibility to share the Good News wherever we go. We are to tell the whole world of Christ's coming, his death on the cross, his resurrection, and his promise to return. Someday each of us will give an account to God regarding how seriously we took this responsibility.[17]

All believers should sense the urgency of witnessing to their family, friends, and acquaintances. If your loved one suffered from a terminal illness and you suddenly discovered the cure for the illness, wouldn't you get the information to him or her as quickly as possible? Along with that, you would do anything possible to encourage your loved one to take advantage of the cure. As believers we have the answer to life. We know how to prevent people from spending an eternity in hell, and we know how to ensure that our loved ones can have a more "abundant life" (see John 10:10). We should not keep this truth to ourselves.

On five occasions Christ gave the Great Commission. In Matthew 28:19–20; Mark 16:15; Luke 24:47–49; John 20:21; and Acts 1:8, Jesus informed his disciples that world evangelization should be the goal of the church. He will help the church find ways to accomplish his command. Now, after approximately two thousand years, we see that the commission could actually be fulfilled in our lifetime. Evangelism is a privilege of being a believer and can be one of the most exciting things we do in life. Committed disciples have determined that they will evangelize by the way they live and the words they choose to use in presenting the gospel.

4. Baptize them.

Warren says of this fourth discipleship purpose,

> In the Greek text of the Great Commission there are three present participle verbs: going, baptizing, and teaching. Each of these is part of the command to "make disciples." Going, baptizing, and teaching are the essential elements of the disciple-making process. At first glance you might wonder why the Great Commission gives the same prominence to the simple act of baptism as it does to the great tasks of evangelism and edification. Obviously, Jesus did not mention it by accident. Why is baptism important enough to warrant inclusion in Christ's Great Commission? I believe it is because it symbolizes one of the purposes of the church: fellowship—identification with the body of Christ.
>
> As Christians we're called to belong, not to just believe. We are not meant to live lone-ranger lives; instead, we are to belong to Christ's family and be members of his body. Baptism is not only a symbol of salvation, it is a symbol of fellowship. It not only symbolizes our new life in Christ.... It says to the world, "This person is now one of us!"[18]

Encouraging new believers to be baptized is critically important. Some have asked, "Is it possible to go to heaven without being baptized?" The answer is "yes" it is possible, but why would a true disciple of Jesus Christ want to disobey the Lord's command to be baptized? Another question: Why would we want to encourage people to neglect something that is God's will for them? Not only does this experience communicate to the church that they are "part of us," but it symbolizes that they are buried with Christ, their sins are washed away, and they are raised to walk a new life in Christ. This experience builds confidence in believers in that they have been obedient to God's will.

5. Teach them to obey.

Warren says,

> The word we commonly use to refer to this purpose is discipleship. The church exists to edify, or educate, God's people. Discipleship is the process of helping people become more like Christ in their thoughts, feelings, and actions. This process begins when a person is born again and continues throughout the rest of his life.... As a church we are called not only to reach people, but also to teach them. After someone has made a decision for Christ, he or she must be discipled. It is the church's responsibility to develop people to spiritual maturity. This is God's will for every believer.... The church exists to edify, encourage, exalt, equip, and evangelize. While each church will differ in *how* these tasks are accomplished, there should be no disagreement about *what* we are called to do.[19]

Discipleship is a process. It is not a sprint, but a lifelong marathon. We are lifelong learners and committed followers. Oswald Chambers said, "In the initial stages of discipleship you get 'stormy weather,' then you lose the nightmare of your own separate individuality and become part of the personality of Christ, and the thought of yourself never bothers you anymore because you are taken up with your relationship to God."[20]

In our desire to witness to others, we must also be aware of the necessity to help them become grounded in their faith if and when they make their choice to become a Christian. One of the most effective ways to ensure that people will not defect from the faith is to help them understand their purpose.

We should feel a sense of responsibility to ensure that those we have led to Christ are becoming growing disciples; however, the responsibility is really twofold. The local church the new disciple attends also has a responsibility to ensure that there are people and programs to encourage the new disciple to grow. This church family should watch over and care for young believers since they are now a part of God's family.

Spiritual Confidence

TO IMPROVE THE ODDS for new disciples to grow in the Christian faith, their confidence that God can be trusted must be built up. Trust comes from a healthy relationship. As new believers understand God and his goodness, they grow into deep relationship with him. Our heavenly Father can be depended on, and he will never forsake any of his children. At the time Martin Luther was experiencing the most intense pressure and trials because of his reformation stand, he said, "Lord, now that you have forgiven me all, do with me as you please."[21] Teen Challenge founder David Wilkerson made this comment about Luther's assuring statement: "Why should I fear what man can do to me? I serve a God who can cleanse me of my iniquity and bring peace to my soul. It doesn't matter if everything around me collapses. If my God is able to save and keep my soul for eternity, why wouldn't he be able to care for my physical body while I'm on this earth? Oh, Lord, now that I'm pardoned, forgiven, and able to stand before you on judgment day with exceeding great joy, do with me as you please!"[22]

Luther's confidence can be the confidence of every Christian. We will go through many trials in life, but we can know that God will be with us in every one of them and enable us to grow through the difficulty we are facing. The Bible gives us numerous assurances as believers. Understanding these assurances builds confidence in the new believer's faith.

Assurance of Salvation

As soon as new Christians make their eternal choice, we need to help them understand what the Scripture says concerning the assurance of salvation. A tremendous starting point is John 6:47: "I tell you the truth, he who believes has everlasting life." Concerning the Scripture, John said, "I write these things to you who believe in the name of the Son of God so that you may know that you have eternal life" (1 John 5:13). Every believer needs to sense this confidence deep within: "God has given us eternal life, and this life is in his Son. He who has the Son has life; he who does not have the Son of God does not have life" (1 John 5:11–12). Assurance to new converts is part of their "faith decision." They must believe the Scripture to be God's promise to them, and then they must make the choice to believe God's eternal guarantees. We, however, must do everything we can to help them understand their assurance of salvation.

Assurance of Forgiveness

The enemy of our souls will most assuredly come back to the new Christian and say, "God didn't really forgive you of all your sins; what you have done is too horrible." Or Satan could say, "You were not sincere enough when you asked God to forgive you; and besides, you have not confessed every sin you have committed." This evil fallen angel Lucifer is also called "the accuser of our brothers" (Rev. 12:10) and will accuse all believers of the sins they have committed. Such an attack can take the wind out of new Christians if they do not have the assurance that all of their sins have been completely forgiven.

John writes, "If we confess our sins, he is faithful and just and will forgive us our sins and purify us from all unrighteousness"

(1 John 1:9). God forgives every repentant Christian, and the deep assurance of his purifying power can be one of the most tremendous truths one can understand. David wrote in Psalm 103:10–12:

> He does not treat us as our sins deserve
>   or repay us according to our iniquities.
> For as high as the heavens are above the earth,
>   so great is his love for those who fear him;
> as far as the east is from the west,
>   so far has he removed our transgressions from us.

Assurance That God Answers Prayer

Prayer is not complicated, mysterious, or difficult; it is simply communicating with God. Language from the heart that expresses our love for God, his goodness, and the requests we are concerned about is all that is required. More than we could ever possibly know, God wants to listen to us and communicate with us. He hears our words, understands the desires of our hearts, and often gives believers an ability to pray in another language (see 1 Cor. 14:2).[23] Knowing that God is always present and ready to listen can take away anxiety, worry, and fear and bring an unsurpassable peace. The Bible tells us, "Do not be anxious about anything, but in everything, by prayer and petition, with thanksgiving, present your requests to God. And the peace of God, which transcends all understanding, will guard your hearts and your minds in Christ Jesus" (Phil. 4:6–7).

When we are concerned about doing the right thing and being obedient to God, we can always approach him with our requests and be assured that he will answer. Jesus said, "I tell you the truth, my Father will give you whatever you ask in my name. Until now you have not asked for anything in my name. Ask and you will receive, and your joy will be complete" (John 16:23–24).

Assurance That the Battle Has Been Won[24]

In our book *The Battle: Defeating the Enemies of Your Soul*, we addressed the tremendous deliverance we have in Christ and the fact that no Christian can be demon possessed. Yesterday I received a telephone call from a pastor. He was broken and on the verge of tears when he called. He said, "I called to thank both of you for writing *The Battle*. I have just finished reading it and feel that I now understand more about the freedom I have in Christ." He explained that he had struggled with the fear that a demon could enter even a Christian, and now he realized that believers are "in Christ" and that Jesus lives within them. There is no possibility that Satan or any of his demons can live in the same "temple" (body) that Jesus lives in. The pastor said he felt a new freedom and boldness to encourage the people he served that they can do "all things through Christ," including defeating the enemy of their souls.

Every born-again believer has been taken from Satan's kingdom and brought into God's. The Bible tells us, "For he has rescued us from the dominion of darkness and brought us into the kingdom of the Son he loves, in whom we have redemption, the forgiveness of sins" (Col. 1:13). This assurance will build tremendous confidence during times of trial or temptation.

Assurance That No Temptation Is Stronger Than Your Faith

Young believers—and longtime believers as well—need to understand that temptation is not sin. Only when we yield to temptation does it develop into sin. D. L. Moody said, "When Christians find themselves exposed to temptation, they should pray to God to uphold them and when they are tempted they should not be discouraged. It is not a sin to be tempted; the sin is to fall into temptation."[25]

I like the story of the little girl who was asked what she did when she was tempted. She said, "Well, when I hear Satan come knocking at the door of my heart, I just say to the Lord Jesus, who lives within my heart, 'Lord Jesus, will You please go to the door?' And then, when the Lord Jesus opens the door, Satan draws away and says, 'Oh! Excuse me, I have made a mistake.'"[26]

Scripture assures us that "no temptation has seized you except what is common to man. And God is faithful; he will not let you be tempted beyond what you can bear. But when you are tempted, he will also provide a way out so that you can stand up under it" (1 Cor. 10:13).

Assurance That God Will Guide Your Life

Today the New Age movement teaches through its occultic doctrine that a person can have a "spirit guide." A so-called chancellor introduces people to the deceased person's spirit, and the spirit is called on to tell them what to do. This is nothing more than twenty-first-century demon possession and demonology. The enemy of our souls would like to confuse innocent people and distract them from the truth. As believers in Christ we are children of God. We can be assured that God will direct our paths if we desire to know his will and depend on him in our decision making. God's eye is on us continually, and he will guide us to live a life of obedience to him. Scripture tells us:

> Trust in the LORD with all your heart
>   and lean not on your own understanding;
> in all your ways acknowledge him,
>   and he will make your paths straight. (Prov. 3:5–6)

JEREMIAH INFORMS US OF God's desire for all believers: "'For I know the plans I have for you,' declares the LORD, 'plans to prosper you and not to harm you, plans to give you hope and a future'" (Jer. 29:11).

Spiritual Optimism

THE CONFIDENCE OF BELIEVERS grows as they understand God's promises. We can encourage those whom we have led to Christ by reminding them of the assurances we have just mentioned and by training them in the discipline of *spiritual multiplication*. Our passion must not only be to tell others about Christ and to see them make decisions to become Christians, but it also must include helping them become solid disciples of Christ. Missiologist David Watson said, "If we were willing to learn the meaning of real discipleship and actually to become disciples, the church in the West would be transformed and the resultant impact on society would be staggering."[27]

America has truly been blessed by God, partly because much of the church in America has been concerned about world evangelization for decades. More missionaries, denominational programs, and parachurch organizations have come from this country than any other country in the history of the church. Nevertheless, we could easily lose our influence because our focus is rapidly changing from substance to style. Discipleship is concerned about substance and depth within an individual believer. Style is concerned with how we look and the fashion of the day. It is surface level, while discipleship is concerned with spiritual maturity. Though we need to be concerned about how we look as a church, the far greater concern should be about how we can take new believers to a depth in Christ where they can become uncompromising disciples.

George Murray of the Evangelical Alliance Mission says there are several concerns we need to have as we face the reality that much of the church in America is losing its cutting edge. Among his "warning alarms" is the fact that a "whole generation of young people are being taught by their Christian parents that their first priority should be to buy a house and build security for the future."

J. Robertson McQuilkin, general editor for the Evangelical Missiological Society, adds,

> Much of evangelical Christianity has bought into the "contemporary cult of self." The typical evangelical church in America has no missions theology and little missions involvement.

In addition, a new Universalism, suggesting that "those who have never heard the gospel are *not* inherently lost," has crept into many evangelical groups, killing world evangelistic motivations.

Ralph Winter, founder of the U.S. Center of World Missions, believes another problem is the breakdown of so many American families. This causes people to focus more on family problems than on world evangelism.

The worst enemy of world evangelism progress, however, is a pervasive pessimism among evangelicals. The prevailing opinion is that the world is getting progressively worse. Yet both history and Scripture bear witness to the fact that the church has grown incredibly in the midst of all kinds of troubles.[28]

How can the church improve the odds of holding people who have professed Christ? The answer resounds through the ages: "Go and make disciples," not "Go and get decisions."

Part Four

Living in Transition

∞ TEN ∞

The Devil's Last Days Strategy

BILLY AND RUTH GRAHAM were on a ministry trip to Paris when someone knocked on their hotel room door. Ruth answered the door and found standing there two men who wanted to give a message to Billy. One explained that the other man was "the Messiah" who had come to see Billy on a "divine errand." Billy Graham's comment on this event was, "After a brief pathetic encounter with another of the deranged people who have come my way claiming to be the Messiah, Ruth remarked to me, 'He claimed to be Christ, but he couldn't even speak to us in our language.' There is a vast menagerie of masquerading messiahs in the world today—both men and women claiming to be Christ. Some of them are mental or emotional cripples. Others scheme and dream with ever more menacing motives and powers. But all of them are counterfeits."[1]

I recently noticed a headline from a New Age magazine that said, "Savior Returns to Earth." Out of curiosity I opened to the page that explained:

> Evidence is mounting that the Christ has returned. He has been appearing miraculously "out of the blue" before large groups throughout Europe, the Middle East, Africa, Asia, Mexico and the United States. He speaks in the local language and then disappears before amazed eyes. . . . Those who have seen him recognize him as their awaited one—Christ for the Christians, the Messiah for the Jews, Maitreya Buddha for the Buddhists, the Ima Mahdi for the Muslims,

and Krishna for the Hindus. Others call him the World Teacher, Maitreya. He comes not as a religious leader, but as a teacher and guide for all humanity.... Hundreds of thousands world wide have seen him.[2]

Several clues of deception in this excerpt ought to stand out to the Christian who has a basic understanding of Christ's return. One is that Jesus clearly warned that believers who are alive in the last days should be careful of deception: "Watch out that no one deceives you. Many will come in my name, claiming, 'I am he,' and will deceive many" (Mark 13:5–6). "At that time if anyone says to you, 'Look, here is the Christ!' or, 'There he is!' do not believe it. For false Christs and false prophets will appear and per- form great signs and miracles to deceive even the elect—if that were possible" (Matt. 24:23–24). In other words, many people will claim they are Jesus Christ, and sadly many will believe some of them.

When Jesus returns to this earth, it will not be to walk among the various religious groups and dialogue with them, nor will it be to show the world that he is the Christ, but he will come to take away his church; believers will meet him in the clouds (see 1 Thess. 4:17).

Another clue is that the author claims this "Christ" is also the Messiah for the Jews, Maitreya Buddha for the Buddhists, the Ima Mahdi for the Muslims, and the Krishna for the Hindus. In other words, he will be the personification of what all religious groups are looking for. But when Jesus returns he will not claim to be the reconciler of all religions nor the "messiah" that various religious groups are waiting for; he will come for those who truly know him as their Lord, and he will come in great power. The enemy of our souls would like the world to think that all religions really are headed for the same place—heaven. This is perhaps one of the greatest deceptions Satan has invented. The truth is that "there is one God and one mediator between God and men, the man Christ Jesus, who gave himself as a ransom for all men" (1 Tim. 2:5–6).

The One World Leader

IN THE LATE '70S WHEN inflation was overwhelming the average worker, Arthur Garcia, forty-three, who supported a wife and five children on a $19,000 per year wage as a worker in U.S. Steel's South Chicago mill, said, "You really want to revolt, but what can you do? I keep waiting for a miracle—for some guy who isn't born yet—and when he comes, we'll follow him like he was John the Baptist."[3]

World leaders and dictators seldom rise to leadership by brute force. Most of the time political upheaval or economic disarray open the door to their entrance. Our complicated, unstable world is prime for a person who will seem to have the answers to international security, world hunger, financial shakiness, and epidemic illnesses. If a person who had this kind of charisma and intellect were introduced today, he would be received with wide-open arms of acceptance.

The Bible tells us there will be such a person. He will have worldwide acceptance as a leader as people place their hopes in his administrative ability. Scripture calls him the "antichrist," which means one who stands against Christ. There is no question that the antichrist will be the greatest deceiver this world has ever known. In fact, the one who inspires him and possesses him will be none other than the "father of lies," the devil himself. Satan will do all he possibly can to convince the world that this person (who will have amazing gifts and supernatural abilities, see Rev. 13:11–17; 2 Thess. 2:1–12) has the talent and insight to become its leader. This attempt by Satan to be worshiped by humankind through the antichrist and to distract people from their Creator God will appear to work; however, it will fail. After seven years of tribulation that will involve the entire world population, the antichrist will actually be thrown alive into hell at the war of Armageddon (see Rev. 19:20).

This world leader could be alive today. Hundreds of years before Christ, Daniel called him "a little" horn (Dan. 7:8), "a stern-faced king, a master of intrigue" (Dan. 8:23), "the ruler who will come" (Dan. 9:26), and "a contemptible person" (Dan. 11:21). Concerning this person, Daniel informs us, "The king will do as he pleases. He will exalt and magnify himself above every god and will say unheard-of things against the God of gods" (Dan. 11:36). In the New Testament, Paul describes this person as "the man of lawlessness" and "the lawless one" (2 Thess. 2:3, 8). His work "will be in accordance with the work of Satan displayed in all kinds of counterfeit miracles, signs and wonders, and in every sort of evil that deceives those who are perishing" (2 Thess. 2:9–10). He is the "beast" of Revelation (13:1) and the ultimate "antichrist" found in the book of First John (1 John 2:18). The Bible gives much information about this individual who will literally rule the world for a short time.

If we are in the final days of the church age, then the prophecies of Scripture concerning the antichrist will soon be fulfilled. George Sweeting, chancellor of Moody Bible Institute, said,

> The world is looking for a powerful leader—an international figure to offer practical solutions to the world's problems of war, suffering, hunger and pestilence. Weary of hollow promises, people want a tried and proven super-leader, a shining knight strong enough to guarantee peace.
>
> In the world today, international leaders change with amazing speed. Looking back over the past ten years, we see that the roster of leaders who were in power ten years ago and still are today is incredibly short. They have been removed from power by resignation, assassination, revolution, and death, and often their power base crumbles with their passing. Those who succeed them often blur their predecessor's achievements and discredit his words; then they fall from power just as quickly.
>
> It is into this kind of political atmosphere that the Antichrist will come. He will offer peace and prosperity, but ultimately he will threaten the very existence of civilization. His power will be so complete and evil that only Jesus Christ

will be able to conquer him and free the world from his grip, thereby bringing down the curtain on the present age.[4]

Through the years many attempts have been made to identify the antichrist, and some people today claim to know who he is. For well over a thousand years projections have come and gone. The list includes various Roman emperors, the leader of the Vandal invaders who sacked Rome, Mohammed, various popes, the papacy itself, Emperor Frederick II and Pope Gregory IX (the last two having viewed each other as the antichrist), Martin Luther, King George II of England, Napoleon Bonaparte, Napoleon III, each side in the American Civil War, Kaiser Wilhelm of Germany, the League of Nations, the United Nations, Hitler, Mussolini, Stalin, King Faisal of Saudi Arabia, Khrushchev, the Soviet Union, Mikhail Gorbachev (the birthmark on his forehead allegedly being the mark of the beast), King Juan Carlos of Spain, Pope John Paul II, Anwar Sadat, the Ayatollah Khomeini, Yassar Arafat, Saddam Hussein, the New Age movement, theologian Matthew Fox, Henry Kissinger, and former president Ronald Wilson Reagan (six letters in each name = 666 [cf. Rev. 13:18], and Reagan recovered from a serious wound [13:3]).[5]

Christians who are alive when the rapture of the church occurs will not know exactly who the antichrist is. We will see the stage set for him (as it is today) and the last attempts of Satan to deceive the world; however, we will be with the Lord when he is ultimately introduced on earth as the one world leader. This strategy of the devil to control all of humankind will perhaps be his most visible scheme, yet he will use many subtle and not-so-subtle deceptive tactics, including counterfeit miracles, during that time. Let's look at some of them.

Diversion of People's Attention from a Literal, Eternal Hell

AS BRIEFLY MENTIONED EARLIER, if the devil can prevent people from thinking or believing in a literal hell, then he also will have taken a great deal of motivation from people to witness and to live a holy life. Satan does not care whether people believe in him, and he especially does not want people to know there is an eternal hell. His goal is to keep people from coming to Christ; whether they become apathetic to spiritual truth or become Satan worshipers makes no difference to him as long as they are in his camp. Satan is very much aware of the short amount of time he has and is willing to use any tactic to "whitewash" hell and slow the evangelism process.

In his classic book *The Screwtape Letters,* C. S. Lewis portrays demons who write each other with their strategies and conversations about people they are attempting to distract from the gospel. One such letter reads,

My Dear Wormwood,

I wonder you should ask me whether it is essential to keep the patient in ignorance of your own existence. That question, at least for the present phase of the struggle, has been answered for us by the High Command. Our policy, for the moment, is to conceal ourselves. Of course this has not always been so. We are really faced with a cruel dilemma. When the humans disbelieve in our existence we lose all the pleasing results of direct terrorism and we make no magicians. On the other hand, when they believe in us, we cannot make them materialists and skeptics. At least, not yet. I have great hopes that we shall learn in due time how to emotionalize and mythologize their science to such an extent that what is, in effect, a belief in us (though not under that name), will creep in while the human mind remains closed to belief in the Enemy. The "Life Force," the worship of sex and some aspects of Psychoanalysis may here prove useful. If once we can produce our perfect work—the Materialist Magician, the man, not using, but veritably worshipping, what he vaguely calls "Forces" while denying the existence of "spirits"—then the end of the war will be in sight. But in the meantime we must obey our orders. I do not think you will have much difficulty in keeping the patient in the dark. The fact that "devils" are predominantly comic figures in the modern imagination will help you. If any faint suspicion of your existence begins to arise in his mind, suggest to him a picture of something in red tights, and persuade him that since he cannot believe in that (it is an old text book method of confusing them) he therefore cannot believe in you.[6]

Satan's goal is to control and destroy, to distract and deceive people from the truth. He does not play fair, he is the father of lies, and he hates you and me. His ultimate goal is to keep people from believing the truth about Jesus Christ and therefore prevent them from going to heaven. He wants everyone to go to hell.[7]

Recently, *USA Today* printed an editorial entitled "Hell Deserves as Much Respect as Heaven." Award-winning writer William R. Mattox wrote,

> Why is our society so schizophrenic about hell? For example, how is it that "hell" is one of the most commonly used words in the English language, yet one of the least-talked about? I mean, go into any sports locker room or military training facility or college night club and you'll hear people use the word "hell" in all sorts of ways—as an interjection, an adjective, a noun.
>
> But try to engage people in any of these settings in a serious conversation about hell, and they'll give you a snooty, raised-eyebrow sort of look that says, "Excuse me, but don't you know it is uncouth to talk about hell in polite conversation?" . . .
>
> Why is it that many people who deny that hell exists also profess belief in heaven? [In survey after survey, at least nine out of ten Americans express belief in heaven while between one-quarter and one-half of all Americans do not believe in hell.] Do these folks really think we will all be together on the other side?[8]

I recently heard about a survey of church members in which it was determined that

10% of the members cannot be found
20% never attend church

25% admit they never pray

35% admit they do not read their Bible

40% admit they never contribute to the church

60% never give to missions

70% never assume responsibility within the church

85% never invite anyone to church

95% have never won anyone to Christ

100% expect to go to heaven[9]

This kind of complacency toward Christian involvement and growth can be one of the most destructive forces the devil uses. If the Enemy cannot keep people from giving their lives to Christ, then he will do all he can to paralyze them so they will not witness for Christ or become involved in God's kingdom. Belief in a literal hell motivates us to do all we can to prevent people from going there.

As a young man I worked in a restaurant for a man named Paul. He was a pastor's son who had chosen to live a terrible life. My father was a pastor, too, and I was always amazed that Paul could grow up in a home where Christianity was so real yet choose to walk away from it. Over the years I lost track of Paul, and I moved a good distance away to Minneapolis to attend college and prepare for the ministry. Surprisingly, one day at a stoplight, I looked at the driver in the car next to me, and it was Paul. I hadn't seen him in years. At that moment, I sensed that the Holy Spirit wanted me to pull over to the side of the road and speak to Paul. I was not obedient because I was in a hurry and the traffic was heavy. I drove off, and then I felt terrible for not being obedient. I thought, "Lord, I've failed you miserably, and if Paul goes into eternity without knowing Jesus Christ, his blood will be on my hands."

For a long time I prayed for him. "Lord, please send somebody to Paul. I have failed you, but send someone to him so that he will know the Lord Jesus Christ."

One day Paul contacted my father. He said, "Tell Tom that I've come back to the Lord, and my wife, Paulie, is serving Christ too." Evidently he knew that I was concerned about his salvation and would want to know. Every once in a while he still writes to let me know he is going on with the Lord.

I thank God that he answers prayer, and I have also determined that I will not miss an opportunity like that again—because hell is real and people without Christ will spend eternity there.

Disillusionment of Demonic Doctrine

DR. JAMES DOBSON RECENTLY WROTE,

> As the Christian church in North America continues to decline and its influence weakens, the nation is falling further into immorality and wickedness. Superstition attracts millions to astrology, psychic readers and ESP. Others are concocting home-made theologies based on everything from New Age nonsense to Eastern mysticism in a search for meaning and security. A large portion of today's younger generation has no memory of the gospel of Jesus Christ and the teachings of Scripture. This is what happens in a culture when the church loses its effectiveness and zeal. We must do everything we can to support this basic institution which God has ordained and blessed.[10]

Dobson has hit the nail on the head. It's as if our society is in a daze, accepting more and more filth through the media, accepting outright attacks against our loving and merciful God, and accepting bold attempts to promote Satanism and witchcraft in sophisticated and attractive ways. It is amazing that so many buy into the Enemy's deception.

Cathy Hainer of *USA Today* writes,

> Bucking a decades-old trend, witches are finally getting some respect.... "Suddenly, witches are younger and cuter, definitely cuter," says entertainment analyst David Davis. "Hollywood is good at picking up on trends. And horror is big right now. By making the witches cuter and more huggable, they can appeal to a larger audience, including women and

younger kids." ... The modern witch hunt isn't just showing up in films. Broom power has come to TV land too. ... The publishing world also is moving full broom-speed ahead with books by, about and for witches. ... "Clearly, society has a desire to look beyond the natural into the supernatural," says Gerald Celente, editor of The Trends Journal. "Whether it's millennium fever or not, a lot of society is pulling away from traditional religions and looking to ancient wisdom. There's a growing interest in astrology, tarot, cabala and paganism, and it's all about a search for inspiration."[11]

Witchcraft, "Wicca" is claimed to be the fastest growing spiritual practice in the USA, with about 400,000 adherents, says Phyllis Currott (a professed participant of Wicca).[12]

The Bible tells us, "The Spirit clearly says that in later times some will abandon the faith and follow deceiving spirits and things taught by demons" (1 Tim. 4:1).

Death Through Persecution

WITH THE GOSPEL SPREADING into more of the world than ever before, more persecution is happening today than during any other time in history. In the twentieth century there were more martyrs for the cause of Christ than in the nineteen prior centuries combined.[13] The people who have gone through persecution have harmed no one, nor have they committed any actual crimes. Today more than two hundred million people in dozens of countries risk being robbed, beaten, raped, imprisoned, or even killed simply because they love Jesus Christ. It's as if the devil is frantically grasping at every means he can to stop the church of Jesus Christ. As John Milton wrote, "Devil: the strongest and fiercest spirit that fought in heaven, now fiercer by despair."[14]

Christ cautioned us that the world would hate us because it first hated him (see John 15:18–20). He also said that "the thief comes only to steal and kill and destroy" (John 10:10), and there is no question that Satan is doing all he can to intimidate, paralyze, and murder people who belong to God. In some parts of the world, Christian women are brutally raped to break their allegiance to Christ, while Christian children are sold into slavery for as little as fifteen dollars. A believer in Bangladesh said, "When my wife was expecting a baby, the Muslim leader took our land and told us not to come back. When we walk through a village, people throw mud at us. We give thanks to God that these things cannot destroy our spirit. Jesus told us that we are only here for a few days. He will take care of all of this."[15]

We must pray for our persecuted brothers and sisters and do all we can to stop such hateful practices. Paul reminds us that all the members of the body of Christ suffer when one member suffers (see 1 Cor. 12:26). In our country it is easy to avoid thinking about the persecuted church, for our persecution is not as intense and few of us face the threat of physical abuse or death. But we must not forget those who are suffering for their faith. Let's look at some of the countries where hateful persecution is taking place.

North Korea

Before the communist takeover, Korea's capital, Pyongyang, was known as "The Second Jerusalem." But a repressive and brutal regime has silenced all but a whisper from Korea's surviving Christian community. One eyewitness account came from a North Korean prisoner who later became a Christian. She reported that Christians in prison camps are singled out for severe treatment, deprived of rest, ordered to recant, beaten, given electric shocks, and assigned the most difficult and dangerous jobs. On top of all this terror, Christians in North Korea suffer from the same devastating famine that afflicts all the people there.

Pakistan

A wave of Islamic fundamentalism in Pakistan has stripped many Christians of their employment, property rights, and educational opportunities. Now they fear for their safety. Christians have been specially targeted by Pakistan's "blasphemy law" and are often falsely accused of blaspheming the prophet Mohammed. No evidence is required, and those convicted face death sentences. In some cases crowds have beaten and killed victims who have not even been formally accused. Christian girls have been abducted and have suffered conversion-by-rape to Islam. Mob attacks on Christians have become sadly common. Christians can expect little help from police, attorneys, or judges, since even they fear the Muslim extremists.

Saudi Arabia

The Islamic nation of Saudi Arabia forbids any expression of Christianity within its own borders while demanding the right to expand Islam abroad. No church buildings, crosses, or religions besides Islam are tolerated in the kingdom. Saudi Islamic police seek out secret worship services by raiding private homes, especially those of visiting workers from less influential countries like India, Egypt, Korea, and the Philippines. The penalty for Christian worship might include lengthy imprisonment without trial, torture, or even death. Yet thriving underground churches here testify to the power of the gospel.

Sudan

In few places is the campaign against Christianity more vicious than in the Sudan. An American Episcopal priest reported, "What we saw and heard and touched is the material for nightmares, a human hell." Already ripped apart by a long civil war, the country is also torn by Jihad led by a militant Islamic regime in Khartoum. Their tactics include aerial bombing of citizens, scorching the earth, destruction of livestock, forced displacement, conscription, abduction, enslavement, imprisonment, torture, and execution— all in the name of Allah.

China

Even as the ruling Communist Party in China makes strides toward a free market economy, it continues to dig in its heels against free religious expression. China's state-sanctioned churches have only the semblance of freedom. In fact, their actions are tightly controlled by the government's Religious Affairs Bureau. Hundreds of Chinese Christians, from evangelical house church members to Roman Catholic priests and bishops, are currently in "reeducation through labor" camps. Many more have been arrested and have not been heard from since.

Nigeria

Historically cordial relations between Nigeria's Christian South and Muslim North have drastically deteriorated since Muslims attempted to introduce Islamic law and Nigeria joined the Organization of the Islamic Conference. Since the 1980s more than six thousand people have been killed in the unrest—mostly Christians. In northern Nigeria the tiny minority of Christians face stringent repression. Building churches is not allowed; using existing churches is often not permitted; and Christians are discriminated against in the educational system.[16]

These countries are only a few of more than seventy countries that the U.S. State Department lists where persecution of Christians is either promoted or permitted, or where existing government policies limit freedom of religion or present potential trouble for Christians and other religious groups.[17] On one occasion Vietnamese Christian To Ding Trung refused early release so that he could minister to the new converts in prison. Most of our brothers and sisters suffer in silence.

Literally millions of Christians meet secretly in house churches in China and other countries because it is illegal for them to meet publicly. Friend, we cannot hide our heads in the sand. Around the world today, Christian persecution is at one of its most horrific levels in history. We must be sensitive to this issue and pray and do all we can to stop such detestable behavior. We can anticipate, however, that Satan will fight us every step of the way until he is finally condemned to an eternal hell with his demonic angels.

In spite of the vicious wave of persecution, one of the greatest signs of the miraculous activity of the Holy Spirit is the ability of Christians to withstand persecution and suffering. *Charisma* magazine reports,

> Many in the West are familiar with the tremendous pressure on Chinese Christians who live under constant threat of imprisonment and torture for their faith. Instead of quashing the church, the intense pressure has purified and strengthened it. Less well known is the plight of Christians in areas such as Israel's West Bank. In this area, whose population is overwhelmingly Palestinian, the chief religion is Islam. Christians, especially converts from Islam who outwardly profess their faith, are in danger of ostracism, imprisonment, and torture. Yet ministers of the gospel are seeing dozens coming to Christ, even at great risk.[18]

Conflict of Complacency

AMERICANS SEEM TO BE in a stupor of complacency concerning the immoral values festering in our nation, including the filth displayed in our entertainment media and the militant promotion of homosexuality. In 1998 homosexual activists claimed that football star Reggie White's statement that homosexuality is a sin ruined his chances of a commentating position with CBS Sports. The Human Rights Campaign (HRC), a gay rights lobbying group, joined other gay rights groups in calling for companies that worked with White to sever their ties to the Green Bay Packers' all-pro defensive lineman. White has endorsed products from several companies, including Campbell Soup and Nike. CBS, meanwhile, announced that it was adding a new show starring radio shock-jock Howard Stern, to its late-night weekend lineup. "'We'll have sex and nudity and lesbians,' says Stern, who's pleased that moral standards are at an all-time low. 'I'm here to represent it. It's a miracle; I prayed to God for this.'"[19]

Gary Bauer of the Family Research Council reports:

Several months ago, the bodies of 54 unborn children were found in a field in Southern California. The children's bodies were dumped in cardboard boxes by an abortion clinic truck driver.

A group of local churches decided the unborn children deserved a proper burial, so they asked the county coroner's office for permission to do that. Last week, some 300 people turned out for a memorial service organized by the churches, and the children were finally laid to rest. By all accounts, it was a moving ceremony that brought attention to the sanctity of human life.

But it almost did not happen. That's because the American Civil Liberties Union threatened to sue, saying that releasing the children for Christian burial violated separation of church and state. A local ACLU leader said, "Under California law, there is only one way to dispose of this material—by incineration."[20]

We are in a war. It's escalating; it's getting bolder; and the Enemy is attacking on every front. Scripture seems to be pointing a finger at today's society when it warns, "There will be terrible times in the last days. People will be lovers of themselves, lovers of money, boastful, proud, abusive, disobedient to their parents, ungrateful, unholy, without love, unforgiving, slanderous, without self-control, brutal, not lovers of the good, treacherous, rash, conceited, lovers of pleasure rather than lovers of God—having a form of godliness but denying its power" (2 Tim. 3:1–5).

Think about this:

- No other nation has killed more babies than the United States has through abortion. We'd rather save the life of a whale than one of our own babies.
- America has the world's highest rate of illegitimate pregnancies.
- Teenage crime in this country is the highest in the free world.

- We have begun to glorify homosexuality and lesbianism. Our media applauds the "bravery" of gays who declare their sexual orientation. Ellen DeGeneres was hailed as a heroine when she came out of the closet as a lesbian on a network television sitcom.

- Network newscasts showed images of half-naked gay women in Florida celebrating "Lesbian Pride Week." An estimated 30,000 lesbians gathered to indulge in drunken orgies day and night for a whole week. Local officials applauded it, saying, "It's wonderful that they're all together here." Radical homosexuals scream at society saying, "In your face!"

- America has brazenly kicked God out of its schools and courts. Now there's even a movement to remove his name from the pledge of allegiance and U.S. coins. People no longer want to hear even the mention of his name.

- A professed "witch" in a city near where I live is using the ACLU to have a "fish" symbol removed from the city's flag. This person does not want any type of Christian symbol on the flag, and the ACLU agrees that this religious symbol is offensive to some people.

- Fifty million Americans now smoke pot, and millions more are hooked on heroin, crack, and other hard drugs.

- Our schools have become bastions of blasphemy and agnosticism. Our children have been robbed of all moral standards and denied all access to God—and they're reacting by becoming more violent and rebellious.[21]

- Eighty percent of the nation's population believes we are in a moral crisis. The Pew Research Organization (April 1997) asked people to list their concerns—what bothers them the most, what worries them the most—and at the top of the list, above everything else, was the decline in moral values.[22]

Our society seems to be ready for whatever the devil has to offer. People are frozen in their complacency and are willing to consider just about any behavior Satan and his demonic forces offer. The only answer is for the church of Jesus Christ to rise up and say "enough is enough" and be the salt of the earth God intended us to be. No satanic attack or activity is as powerful as the church. We are the only true "light" in an increasingly dark world. The more we are willing to take a stand for righteousness and the more people we evangelize for God's kingdom, the less influence the Enemy will have on our world.

Devastation of Divorce

THE MOST POWERFUL INSTITUTION on earth is the church of Jesus Christ—born-again believers who have a living relationship with Jesus Christ. The Enemy attacks "the church," not any particular denominational group. He wants to destroy or paralyze a believer's faith in whatever way he can. One of the most obvious ways the Enemy can attack a person's faith is by attacking his or her marriage and family. A Christian marriage is a powerful witness to a hurting world, and when Satan can ruin a marriage, he can take much of a believer's strength. This is why I believe that Christian marriages are suffering much like non-Christian marriages. God hates divorce (see Mal. 2:16) because he loves people and hates the pain that divorce brings to families. Anything God hates, Satan loves. Anything God loves, Satan hates.

Today's marriages are in trouble, both inside and outside the church.

After interviewing 3,142 randomly selected adults across the nation, including 1,220 born-again Christians, statistician George Barna discovered,

- One out of every four adults (24%) who has been married has experienced a divorce.
- Born-again Christians are slightly more likely than non-Christians to go through a divorce. Twenty-seven percent of Christians have seen their marriages break up, compared to 23% of non-Christians.

- Adults who describe themselves as Christian fundamentalists are more likely than others to get divorced: 30% have experienced divorce.

- Based on data comparing the ages at which people were married and at which they accepted Christ as their Savior, we found that accepting Christ does not reduce the incidence of divorce. Among adult Christians who have ever been divorced, 87% experience their divorce after accepting Christ as their Savior.[23]

Needless to say, numerous well-known ministry leaders encouraged the Barna research group to double check its findings. Upon further research the results were the same. The fact remained, Christians are every bit as likely as are non-Christians to be devastated by divorce.[24]

Over the years we have worked with countless couples going through divorce. We have witnessed the personal pain, heartache, and shame that comes to a believer who has had this experience. Much of the time it is because of sinful behavior on the part of one or both of the partners. At times it is because of people with hardened hearts who refuse to do what they should to repair the relationship. Whatever the cause, incredible agony comes to the home. The ability to live a victorious Christian life is greatly damaged while the individuals are trying to heal, and there is no question that Satan has won a great victory. If for no other reason besides our Christian witness and our love for God, we must stand for our marriage and do all we can to grow in our relationship with our spouse.

Disillusionment of Jesus' Promised Return

PERHAPS ONE OF THE most subtle devices Satan will use in the last days will be his efforts to remove the hope that Christians have concerning the rapture of believers from this earth and the second coming of Jesus Christ. Peter cautioned,

You must understand that in the last days scoffers will come, scoffing and following their own evil desires. They will say,

"Where is this 'coming' he promised? Ever since our fathers died, everything goes on as it has since the beginning of creation." ... But do not forget this one thing, dear friends: With the Lord a day is like a thousand years, and a thousand years are like a day. The Lord is not slow in keeping his promise, as some understand slowness. He is patient with you, not wanting anyone to perish, but everyone to come to repentance (2 Peter 3:3–4, 8–9).

There is a great lack of preaching from today's pulpits about the rapture of the church and Christ's return. Seldom does the topic come up in the typical Christian's conversations, yet the subject of his return is a frequent subject in the Bible. Satan does not want us to have this kind of hope. He knows that when people look forward to the day when they will be taken from this earth and the time when Jesus Christ will return to rule the earth, they will be more motivated to live a holy life and tell others about Christ. He wants to hide this truth from as many as possible.

When news anchor Peter Jennings was reporting on the persecution of Christians in China, he pointed out that many evangelical leaders in America are (rightfully) applying pressure on the Clinton administration to persuade the president not to renew most-favored-nation trade status with China because of the government's cruel persecution of Christians. Just in passing, Peter Jennings added a startling observation. He said, "There is only one doctrine the Chinese government will not allow the official churches to preach, and that is the doctrine of the Second Coming of Christ."[25] Why? Perhaps they understand that when Jesus returns, he will establish his kingdom over all the earth and overthrow all other political systems. This thought may be frightening to Chinese leaders, as they will be one of the systems Christ will overthrow.

Perhaps the most tragic issue is that in "free" America pastors and leaders are simply not talking about Christ's return. We need to understand that this truth will encourage believers as little else. The Enemy wants us to be blind to this truth or not think about it.

Our Hope

THE DEVIL NEVER PLAYS fair; he is involved in guerrilla warfare and will do anything in his power to distract people from the truth. He will attempt to discourage us, accuse us, and tempt us to fail God. As the day approaches when Satan realizes that his time is short, he will intensify his efforts. In our book *The Battle: Defeating the Enemy of Your Soul*, we describe in more detail his tactics and how we can have victory over evil.

We must always remember that "the one who is in [us] is greater than the one who is in the world" (1 John 4:4). Peter wrote to the early Christians that the "devil prowls around like a roaring lion looking for someone to devour" (1 Peter 5:8); however, Peter added these powerful words: "Resist him, standing firm in the faith" (v. 9). As Satan's tactics and devices increase and it seems that you are in a constant battle that will not end, tell yourself that "with God's help, I am going to make it!" And then, stand in your trust in Jesus Christ. Our powerful God will never permit anything to come to your life that you cannot handle. The Scripture tells us that "God is faithful; he will not let you be tempted beyond what you can bear. But when you are tempted, he will also provide a way out so that you can stand up under it" (1 Cor. 10:13). Oswald Chambers said, "The devil is a bully, but when we stand in the armor of God he cannot harm us; if we tackle him in our own strength, we are soon done for; but if we stand with the strength and courage of God, he cannot gain one inch of way at all."[26]

Though the enemy of our souls is working as never before, I've never been more excited about the future. Think about it: God has destined us to live during this incredible time in history. Do not fear the devil, but put all of your trust in the One who defeated Satan two thousand years ago on the cross. Also, do all you can to tell those close to you that they can have hope.

ELEVEN

The Millennial Mandate

F EW WOULD DOUBT WE are living in a world that is adrift. Large
population groups are moving from city to city and from country to country looking for stability. They are desperate and willing
to settle anywhere they can find security. Billy Graham says,
"Decay in the societies of the world, consternation in the governments, and a deep heart-cry for revival throughout the Church of
our Lord Jesus Christ all point to the need of the world for our
Savior."[1] Missiologist Donald McGavran feels that such times of
transition provide the best moments to lead people to God
through Jesus Christ.[2] If there has ever been a time of transition,
uncertainty, and disorder, it is today. Yet the church is called to
hold steady, remain hopeful, and "press on" in spite of worldwide
turmoil.

As we pass the year 2000, we can anticipate an epidemic of
date setters trying to pinpoint the end of this world as we know it,
or endeavoring to set the exact time when Christ will return to the
earth. Similarly, this happened as the church approached the year
1000. The present-day hysteria around the Y2K dilemma is being
used as an example of how the world could be thrown into
upheaval and chaos. The most common prediction is that we are
going to experience a computer meltdown on December 31, 1999,
due to computers and their software not being able to handle
dates in the new millennium. Some have even warned that trains,
planes, ships, and automobiles may suddenly quit working. The
same people speculate that bank accounts will be deleted

overnight; electrical generating plants will shut down; the whole economy will be thrown into confusion; looting will break out; and society will respond with panic and survival tactics.

We must remind ourselves that people have historically endeavored to predict the time of Christ's return and have even resorted to bizarre arguments to support their view. Some of the ideas we have heard in the last few years: "The buzzards are gathering in Israel"; "The ark of the covenant has been found"; "The building blocks of the temple have been cut and are presently being stored in K-Marts"; and "The planets are going to line up" (which will affect the gravitational pull of the earth). A widely distributed book entitled *88 Reasons Why Jesus Will Return in 88* carried a number of strange predictions that came and went with time, and those who used these examples as they witnessed were a little red-faced.

Nevertheless, as we approach the time when Christ will take the church from the earth, we will see signs of his return. As we have written in chapter 10 above, there are more signs today than ever before. We can say with confidence that we are in the season of his return. That, however, is much different than setting dates or coming up with silly examples of why it's going to happen this year, next year, or whatever year.

More than the feared computer meltdown, I watch the condition of people's hearts. Satan has a global strategy for deceiving humankind and setting up the antichrist's regime. He is getting bolder and bolder as his day of reckoning approaches. The hideous "legal right" of people to murder millions of unborn children each year is his attempt to desensitize us to the preciousness of human life. The militant homosexual agenda that promotes its form of sexuality as an "alternative lifestyle" is his attempt to mock God's standards of holiness and the uniqueness of men and women. His inspiration of destructive "false ministers" who promote themselves and invent false doctrine is his attempt to make people wonder *What is the truth?* The genocide that has occurred in Albania, Yugoslavia, parts of Africa, and in the past in Germany and Russia as well as numerous other places is his attempt to cause people to feel despair and ignore human suffering. The persecution and murder of God's precious saints are Satan's attempts to convince people that he can do whatever he pleases to God's church.

Satan's hideous assaults are going to increase, so we must constantly remind ourselves that we do not belong to this world (see John 15:19; 1 Peter 2:11); Jesus Christ dwells in us and we in him (see Rom. 8:10; Eph. 3:17; Col. 2:6–7). As Paul said, "I can do everything through him who gives me strength" (Phil. 4:13).

In the fall of 1998 the blasphemous play *Corpus Christi* opened in New York City. In this play Jesus is depicted as a homosexual, having a sexual affair with Judas and his other disciples. On stage the man who plays Jesus places a "wide-mouthed" kiss on Judas's lips. Friend, this is crucifying afresh the Son of God, our wonderful Savior. People were lining up and paying for expensive tickets to see this bold attempt of Satan to mock the Son of God.

In a 1997 *Charisma* magazine article entitled "Invasion from the Dark Side," George Otis wrote that on Labor Day weekend in 1996, Nevada's Black Rock Desert turned into a "hell-themed" hotbed of demonic activity. Up to ten thousand "spiritual nomads" (many of them former Christians) from over twenty countries converged to blaspheme, rebel, and worship Satan.

This pagan, hell-bent festival for the sacrilegious featured theme camps such as Motel 666 and an attraction called "Crucifixion with a Celebrity," where visitors could have their pictures taken hanging next to a chubby Elvis. At McSatan's Bistro God was challenged to consume sinners with brimstone.

Saturday night's drama was the weekend's highlight. Meant to depict hell with "Papa Satan" as special guest, its parade of Christian mockery pictured hell on earth through lechery, nudity, malevolence, seduction, and copulation.[3]

I'm afraid the day is rapidly approaching when America will have gone too far. Judgment is right at the door.

When will such blatant sin end? Not until Jesus Christ comes back with his saints at the end of the tribulation. It will be over

without a shot being fired from God's people and will be the short-
est world war that humankind will experience. As God spoke this
world into existence (see Gen. 1), so too, Jesus Christ will end the
battle with a "sword" that will come out of his mouth (see Rev.
19:21).

Instead of becoming prophets of doom and becoming paralyzed by predictions of worldwide chaos, we ought to become
stirred up in our faith and do all we can to bring people to Christ.
This is a day when people are searching for the truth and perhaps
are more open than any time in history. As believers we have
Christ in our lives and can overcome this world in spite of the
tremendous onslaught of the Enemy. Like no other time in history, we face both danger and opportunity. The danger is that we
will not join together to seize the incredible opportunity to reach
a very unstable, confused world that is desperately looking for
answers.

The Greatest Darkness Comes Just Before the Dawn

IN SPITE OF THE darkness, this could be the greatest day for the
church of Jesus Christ. The twentieth century saw tremendous
growth in the church as Christianity moved throughout the world.
David Barrett, a research professor of missiometrics, reported in
Christianity Today,

Percentage of evangelical Christians compared to general population

	1900	1998
North America	14%	27%
Latin America	4%	14%
Europe	12%	23%
Africa	3%	13%
Asia	1%	5%
Oceania	9%	28%[4]

The evangelical church is growing faster in many parts of the
world than is the world's population.

Growth since 1970

	Population	Evangelicals
World	60%	126%
Europe	11%	41%
North America	31%	57%
Oceania	53%	93%
Africa	114%	207%
Latin America	76%	233%
Asia	67%	326%[5]

Author and church historian Mark Hutchinson says,

About one-third of the world's population has some allegiance to Christianity, and about 700 million of these are what researcher David Barrett calls "Great Commission" Christians. These are Christians who believe in the centrality of the Cross, in Jesus Christ as Savior, the Bible as God's Word, and in the mandate to spread the gospel. It is to these Christian believers I am referring when I speak of evangelical Christians. Of these evangelical Christians, more than half are charismatic or Pentecostal.... Pentecostalism is the largest and most dynamic movement within evangelicalism.[6]

The twenty-first century will likely see greater growth, revival, and worldwide evangelization than even the twentieth century. God will use this time of uncertainty to speak through us to people who are desperately searching for meaning and relationships. He will use the church of Jesus Christ to speak to a frightened, disillusioned, confused world that stability, meaning, and peace can be found only through Jesus Christ.

The young people who will bridge across the millennium are called "bridgers." They are also called "the millennial generation." Charles Dunahoo writes, "The church's challenge—reaching the millennials. These kids do not ask their friends, 'What does your dad do?' but 'Do you have a dad?' and if so, 'Do you know your dad?' or perhaps, 'How many dads do you have?'"[7]

Many bridgers have grown up with dysfunctional families (the boomers and busters) and are misunderstood by sociological experts. While they might seem rebellious, uncaring about career goals, and radical—deep down inside they are looking for meaning. Bridgers want stable relationships. It's no wonder, since this is a basic need within all of us. They have grown up watching relationships being shattered, and they hunger for relationships that will stay intact. Because of the instability of this world—and their own private world—few of them attend church. Out of the 72 million bridgers, only 4 percent are thought to be Christians.[8]

How are we going to win the bridgers? They need to hear teaching and preaching that will connect them in a relational way to Christ and his community, the church. They need to see Christian people who truly live out their faith and demonstrate *koinonia* (fellowship, relationship). This should not be that big of a hurdle since Christianity is relational. The personal relationship with Jesus Christ is our stability, and our relationships within the body of Christ are meant to be a constant encouragement to our well-being.

The Job Is Doable

FOR THE FIRST TIME in the history of the Christian church, the completion of the Great Commission is within our reach. The fire of passion in people's hearts to see the task finished is growing. Jesus never would have given the command to make disciples of all the nations if he thought for a moment that his followers could not do it.[9] We can now see the possibility and can sense that the time is near. Anticipation is growing worldwide. Denominations, parachurch groups, churches, and individuals are beginning to talk about how to finish the assignment our Leader gave two thousand years ago.

The only reason to doubt that our generation will not see the task finished is if we lose our vision. Complacency and discouragement are the twin enemies of vision. Billy Graham says, "Complacency makes us lazy; discouragement paralyzes us. With 70 percent of the world not even claiming to know Christ, we can't afford to be com-

placent. When God is still at work, we dare not get discouraged."[10]
We cannot list all of the groups that are focused on finishing the task,
but here we list a few that we feel you may become aware of and perhaps involved in.

Worldwide Prayer Movements

As never before, individuals and people from numerous
denominational groups and parachurch organizations are praying
for world evangelization. In our book *The Battle: Defeating the
Enemies of Your Soul*, we write,

> The evangelical scholar J. Edwin Orr summarized, into
> one statement, his sixty years of historical study on great
> prayer movements preceding spiritual awakenings. He says,
> "Whenever God is ready to do something new with his
> people, he always sets them to praying." If this is true and
> foundational to God's agenda when revival is on the horizon,
> then a worldwide revival is coming. The most hopeful sign of
> our times is the prayer movement.
>
> David Barrett . . . has gathered the following statistics:
>
> - Worldwide there are about 170 million Christians who
>   are committed to praying daily for world evangeliza-
>   tion and spiritual awakening (revival).
> - Of this group, twenty million believe that praying for
>   world revival is the primary calling that God has given
>   them. They are what we call "prayer warriors."
> - Around the world are at least ten million prayer groups
>   that have a common focus in prayer each time they meet.
>   They continually ask God to bring worldwide revival.
> - Worldwide there are an estimated thirteen hundred
>   prayer mobilization networks endeavoring to persuade
>   the church to pray more for world revival.
>
> David Bryant, an evangelical prayer movement leader,
> commented on this modern-day phenomenon respecting
> prayer: "If we know historically, as Dr. Orr suggests, this
> groundswell of prayer is a gift of God; if it is biblically accu-
> rate to teach that God has not only ordained the end but also

the means (the end being world revival, the means being the prayers of his people); if this massive chorus of prayer is increasingly focused on nothing less than national and world revival; and if, when God stirs us up to this type of praying he does so because he is actually ready to answer us—how can we believe otherwise than that world revival is bearing down on top of us?"[11]

Not long ago over 30 million people prayed for new ways and more people to reach those who live in what is called the "10/40 Window." This geographical location is where nearly half of the world's population live and where ninety-seven percent of those least touched by the gospel live. Today most Pentecostal, evangelical, and interdenominational groups are seeking ways to reach this part of the world, and as a result, tremendous things are beginning to happen. God is showing missions organizations, denominations, and individuals ways to reach these masses, and because so many are praying, we often hear of miraculous occurrences that have opened the heart of an individual or a community to the gospel.

In Bangladesh, which is within the 10/40 Window, a medical team called HealthCare Ministries[12] recently responded to a crisis. As the doctors and professional medical staff provided medical assistance for the people, they also told each person about the gospel of Jesus Christ. As they were sharing the plan of salvation with a 113-year-old Muslim, he said that he had never heard of Jesus, but on that day he quickly accepted Christ as his Savior. Afterward he explained that when he was 100 years old, he had a dream of a man who said, "Someone will come and explain to you the way to God." With deep emotion he said, "You have just fulfilled that dream."

Evangelist Luis Palau related miraculous events that Pastor Menes Abdul Noor of Cairo, Egypt, has witnessed with people in the Middle East. Noor said,

> Every Arabic Christian I have talked to who converted to Christ from a non-Christian background relates a dream or vision in which Jesus, dressed in white as in the Transfig-

uration, speaks directly to them, telling them he is the Savior of the world. A woman whose father is a top leader in her nation—a nation where there are no church buildings—was converted through a dream in which Jesus revealed himself. The first five years of her Christian life she didn't even have a Bible.

Christians in the Middle East, many of whom are respected professionals with postgraduate degrees, expect God to work in this way. They believe in his supernatural intervention. If God is God, he is going to do supernatural things. No barriers can thwart or frustrate God's redemptive plan.[13]

Pastor Ted Haggard of New Life Church in Colorado Springs spoke of a missionary named David Hogan who ministers in rural Central and South America. His goal is to locate villages that currently have no gospel church, go there, preach, pray for miracles, and establish a local church. Haggard explains that Hogan experiences "regular vivid demonstrations of deliverance and remarkable spiritual phenomena." In some regions of Central America, family members will not bury their dead until one of David's missionaries has come and prayed for them. There are more than 150 documented instances of people being raised from the dead. As a result, Haggard says, "thousands of villages that didn't have a church, now have a church of people who believe the Bible and worship God."[14]

Charisma magazine reports,

Spectacular things are happening in the church around the world. Miracles, healings, prophetic revelations and spectacular church growth across the globe are evidence to many that the Holy Spirit is working on a grand scale.

In a most dramatic example, the church in China has grown by tens of millions in the last 20 years. This growth has been attributed to miraculous occurrences. Even skeptical neighbors and family members have been led to faith after witnessing the supernatural work of God, manifested in an outpouring of divine healings and in changed lives.[15]

Healings and other miracles in other countries have also brought many to believe. "In Mexico a nation-wide revival of Pentecostal power has been evidenced by healings on a mass scale."[16] Tremendous breakthroughs are happening in regions of the world where the gospel previously had not had much success.

In Iceland, an island nation which inherited not only the spirited independence of the Vikings but also the spiritual oppression of paganism, the church is seeing many conversions and answers to prayer. In answer to one particular prayer, God provided a 5,000-watt transmitter for a Reykjavik businessman to start a Christian television station. Now the majority of Icelanders are able to hear the gospel regularly. In Macedonia, which has been traditionally unreceptive to the gospel, God is using a Swedish mission organization to establish churches, preschools, and clinics. Churches have burgeoned as the gospel is distributed daily with compassion. The Swedish leaders were invited to lay hands on Macedonia's first president and pray a blessing over him.[17]

In the African nation of Benin, President Matthew Kerekou, a former communist dictator, has dedicated his nation to Christ and is an outspoken advocate of evangelical Christianity.

Missiologist George Otis Jr. says that

out of all the people who have been saved since the time of Christ,

- 70% have been saved since 1900.
- 70% of those have been saved since 1945.
- 70% of those have been saved in the last 10 years.[18]

Momentum is building because people are praying. Prayer is perhaps the greatest key we have to finishing the task of reaching the world for Christ. As Christians watch the world's population grow and the Enemy endeavors to prevent people from coming to the truth, believers are praying for God to give them boldness, creativity, and enablement to finish the task.

Unparalleled Cooperation and Technological Tools

DENOMINATIONAL AND PARACHURCH GROUPS are joining together to pray and to strategize together about finishing the task of taking the gospel to the entire world. David Bryant is certain that when the church throughout the world prays for revival, God will respond. He said that a primary reason for hope is found in the growth of "revival prayer" throughout the world. National days of prayer, citywide prayer events, youth prayer groups, prayer training ministries—these and many more activities indicate a fresh fervency for prayer. Bryant feels that such fervency is not natural; it is a gift from God. We do not naturally seek God. We do not naturally pursue the Holy Spirit. We do not naturally cross denominational and ethnic lines to pray together. The only explanation is that God is stirring his people to pray, and such prayers will not go out in vain. We have strong reason for hope, for if we want revival, imagine how much more God wants it—and he can bring it to pass![19]

This cross-denominational cooperation is demonstrated not only in prayer but through other profound cooperative efforts as well. For example, numerous denominational groups and Christian organizations have endeavored to utilize *The Jesus Film Project*, developed by Campus Crusade for Christ, as a witnessing tool to be used throughout the world. This amazing tool has had powerful results. Campus Crusade reports that as of July 1998, 1,623,129,222 people had seen the film, and as a result 83,426,023 people had made decisions for Christ. The Jesus film has been shown in 223 countries. Because of the tremendous response, Campus Crusade has organized 2,174 project teams that facilitate the film and present a closing response time for the viewers, during which they can make a commitment to Christ.[20] The film is now available in 349 languages, and plans are in place to make it available in 1,156 languages, or to 98 percent of the world's population.[21]

Another phenomenal evangelism effort is *Evangelism Explosion*. Author and pastor of the fastest-growing Presbyterian church in America, D. James Kennedy developed this easy to understand and effective one-to-one witnessing program. To date more than 100,000 churches in 211 countries are utilizing his format to involve people in witnessing and leading others to Christ.[22]

Mission America is a growing coalition of more than 350 national Christian leaders of denominations, churches, and ministries seeking to mobilize the church to pray for and share the gospel of Jesus Christ with every man, woman, young person, and child in America by the end of the year 2000. The goal is to fulfill the Great Commission within America. Never before in the history of the American church have so many members of the body of Christ come together for the purpose of evangelism.[23]

The *American Bible Society* is committing $5 million to a project intended to link every church in the United States and Canada to the World Wide Web. Houses of Worship is an Internet site that will network more than 300,000 churches in North America for increased dialogue, cooperation, and publicity. Just as churches pioneered the invention and use of the printing press, today's churches and religious leaders are pioneering a new positive use of the Internet to connect and spread their messages.[24]

Reinhard Bonnke is perhaps one of the greatest evangelists to Africa today. He has begun a program created to distribute his booklet *The Epic of Christ's Cross* to millions of people. The message of the cross and the plan of salvation are given in the book. In 1994–97 he gave the booklet to 80,280,000 homes in numerous countries outside the United States. During Easter week 1999, the same book, retitled *Beyond 99*, was sent to 125 million homes in the United States and Canada.

The missions organization *Youth With A Mission* is comprised mainly of young adults from various evangelical denominations who want to give a short time (from a few months to two years) to missions work. As of January 1998 they had 28,000 short-term staff and more than 10,000 permanent staff. They have 586 centers located in 132 nations. These young people are powerfully impacting the world for God's kingdom.

The *Billy Graham Evangelistic Association* is not only utilizing Graham's crusades to evangelize the lost; it has also created a host of other programs to fulfill the Great Commission. The association has developed the Billy Graham Training Center (The Cove), which is a unique training center designed to equip ordinary Christians with the extraordinary capacity to reach people effectively for Christ. Other ministries include Schools of Evangelism, *Decision* magazine, World Wide Pictures, crusade telecasts (with telephone ministry), and Graham's numerous books, many of them geared to reach the lost. Much of what the Billy Graham Evangelistic Association does is interdenominational and intended to help Christian churches work together for the purpose of evangelism. Billy Graham's son, Franklin, who is the president of Samaritan's Purse, is involved in relief efforts throughout the world. Samaritan's Purse recently sent more than 2.2 million shoe boxes stuffed with Christian literature and gifts for needy children in fifty-five countries during the Operation Christmas Child outreach.

The ministry *Convoy of Hope,* a national food and evangelistic ministry, is focused on cooperating with interdenominational groups for the purpose of ministering to the urban poor. Convoy of Hope provides citywide events that mobilize volunteers to shower inner-city neighborhoods with fun, food, and the gospel.

During the last week of 1999, churches will unite with Convoy of Hope in an event called "We Care, L.A." It is anticipated that thousands of volunteers will blitz Los Angeles with acts of kindness. Christians will visit hospitals; clean up parks; paint buildings; comfort the lonely; and deliver free groceries, toys, and clothing. This ministry thrives on ministry to those who are often ignored. One of their goals is to "make the inner-city pastor a hero in his community." Convoy of Hope has distributed over 5 million pounds of food to more than 300,000 people in most American cities since its inception in 1995. Over 80,000 people have become Christians at makeshift altars where convoys have been held.[25]

To finish the task of world evangelization, Pentecostal, evangelical, and parachurch groups must network. We cannot do it alone; we need each other. Those who love Jesus Christ with all of their hearts must join hands with the united focus of finishing the task.

The main reason world evangelization plans fail is poor planning and lack of leadership, according to *700 Global Plans to Evangelize the World* by David Barrett and James Reapsome. The book evaluates plans implemented from A.D. 30 up to the present and concludes that cooperation and communication among leaders are critical factors. Of the fourteen denominations and parachurch organizations that set global evangelism goals in 1990, most did not network with the others.[26]

Thankfully, there seems to be a commitment from a growing number of evangelical leaders to work together for the sake of the lost. As author Neil Anderson says, "Globally, the Holy Spirit has woven together a massive cooperative effort that could produce a harvest of at least one billion souls in the next five years. The church could be experiencing the first fruits of the greatest awakening it has ever known."[27]

People around the world can hear the gospel message on radio in 255 languages, and Christian television is also reaching much of the world. In 1994 a Billy Graham crusade was sent to a billion people by satellite. Bible translators have been able to provide New Testaments in 1,165 languages. In just a few hours, the gospel can get into the neediest locations in the world. Most of the globe can be reached by telephone. We have the tools today to go where we have never been able to go, do what we have never been able to do, including getting right into a person's living room.

Because of the educational opportunities in the United States, tens of thousands of people from other nations are coming to America for their professional training. Immigration opens the doors for some of the most difficult to reach ethnic groups to come to us. We can take advantage of all these opportunities as we work together to finish a task that is now doable.

New Millennium, Same Gospel

I AM MORE EXCITED about the possibilities we have to reach the world for Christ than ever before. Yes, there is good reason to be concerned for the world. We must do all we can to protect the earth; feed and care for those who are in need; and protect the unborn, the disabled, and the elderly. We must find ways to protect people from terrorist activity and religious persecution. Christians must be "salt and light" in a very dark world as we are driven by the understanding that Jesus Christ is the answer for every human being. Church historian Kenneth Scott Latourette writes that throughout its history "the primary emphasis of the Church was upon the salvation of the individual for eternal life." The great nineteenth-century British preacher Charles H. Spurgeon believed that "the work of conversion is the first and great thing we must drive at; after this we must labor with all our might." John Wesley reminded preachers, "You have nothing to do but to save souls."[28]

Evangelist Luis Palau says,

> The evangelical Christians of North America cheerfully pay any amount to go to a concert. They fill the civic center for worship sessions and even intercessory spiritual-warfare conventions. But when it comes to face-to-face warfare, which is talking to people kindly but directly about their need for Christ, suddenly the numbers diminish. In too many churches the response to the challenge to proclaim the gospel to their city is, "Why should we be doing this?" and "This is expensive."[29]

WHEN WE THINK OF the lostness of people without Christ, nothing is too expensive.

Will you choose to speak to someone about Christ? Will you determine to ask that person to make a decision? And if that person makes a commitment to give his or her life to Jesus, will you endeavor to do all you can to ensure that that person becomes a faithful disciple? Evangelism is as basic as that. When we, together, decide to reach our world one at a time, the task of world evangelism will be finished rapidly.

People are watching you. Because of your Christian example, you could be asked by an employee, employer, neighbor, friend, or relative about the Christ you serve. Have you chosen to be the greatest witness you can possibly be? Have you chosen to tell someone about Jesus Christ? If we work together, the job is doable. "This gospel of the kingdom will be preached in the whole world as a testimony to all nations, and then the end will come" (Matt. 24:14).

Notes

Introduction

1. W. Charles Arn, "Our Unchurched Neighbors," *Leadership* 17, no. 2 (Spring 1996), 75.

2. James Kraus, "Church Attendance Drops to Lowest Level in Two Decades," *The Church Around the World* 27, no. 1 (December 1996), 2.

3. Justin Long, "North America: Decline and Fall of World Religions, 1900–2025," *Monday Morning Reality Check*, 23 February 1998, 1–3: quoted in *Current Thoughts and Trends*, June 1998, 26.

4. "The Boom of Buddhism," *Christian Science Monitor*, 3 November 1997, 9: quoted in *Current Thoughts and Trends*, June 1998, 26.

5. Carla Power, "The New Islam," *Newsweek* 131, no. 11 (16 March 1998), 34–37: quoted in *Current Thoughts and Trends*, June 1998, 26.

6. Mary Rourk, "Many Keep the Faith(s) in 'New' U.S.," *Los Angeles Times:* quoted in "More Americans Keeping a Different Faith Nowadays," *Philadelphia Inquirer*, 5 July 1998, E1.

7. In part, the answer to the question of why the Muslim, Buddhist, and other religious groups are growing in America could be because of demographics. More Muslims, Buddists, and people of other religions are entering the United States each year and maintaining their religious affiliation. Statistics also show, however, that these religions are growing because of converts.

8. George Barna, "The American Witness," *Barna Report*, November/December 1997, 2.

9. Ibid., 7.

10. George Barna, "Reaching Without Preaching," *Barna Report*, Premiere Issue, 1.

11. Author unknown.

12. William Barclay, *The Acts of the Apostles* (Philadelphia: Westminister Press, 1976), 90.

13. Mary Adamski, "At Lolani Palace, the Kalaupapa Cleric Is Called a Friend and Crusader," *Honolulu Star Bulletin*, 15 July 1995.

14. Ibid.

15. This experience happened to Wayde I. Goodall.

16. George Barna, "Views of Evangelicals on Life and Faith," *Barna Report* 1, no. 5, 3.

17. William Barclay, *The Letters to the Corinthians* (Philadelphia: Westminister Press, 1975), 185.

18. Ibid., 187.

19. This experience happened to Thomas E. Trask.

20. Billy Graham, "Recovering the Primacy of Evangelism," *Christianity Today* 4, no. 14 (8 December 1997), 27–30: quoted in *Current Thoughts and Trends,* February 1998, 11.

21. Helmut Thielicke: quoted in *Ministry Advantage* 7, no. 3 (Summer 1997), 3.

22. H. B. London, *The Pastor's Weekly Briefing* 6, no. 17 (23 April 1998), 1: quoted in Barna Research Group news release of 20 April 1998.

23. Graham, "Recovering the Primacy of Evangelism": quoted in *Current Thoughts and Trends,* February 1998, 11.

24. Edythe Draper, *Draper's Book of Quotations for the Christian World* (Wheaton, Ill.: Tyndale, 1992), 64.

Chapter One—What Do You Value Most?

1. Judith Couchman, *Corrie ten Boom: Anywhere He Leads Me* (Ann Arbor, Mich.: Servant, 1997), 146.

2. Ibid., 147.

3. Edythe Draper, *Draper's Book of Quotations for the Christian World* (Wheaton, Ill.: Tyndale, 1992), 300.

4. James Patterson and Peter Kim, *The Day America Told the Truth* (New York: Plume, 1992), 37.

5. Ibid., 26–27.

6. Ibid., 26.

7. Draper, *Quotations,* 359.

8. Henry H. Halley, *Halley's Bible Handbook* (Grand Rapids: Zondervan, 1965), 620.

9. Draper, *Quotations,* 359.

10. Annie Johnston Flint, "He Giveth More Grace," in Ravi Zacharias, *Cries of the Heart* (Dallas: Word, 1998), 74.

11. Malcolm Muggeridge: quoted in Donald McCullough, *Waking from the American Dream* (Downers Grove, Ill.: InterVarsity Press, 1988), 145.

12. Draper, *Quotations,* 616.

13. Ibid., 625.

14. Dwight L. Moody, *Notes from My Bible* (Chicago: Revell: 1895), 172.

15. George Sweeting, *Great Quotes and Illustrations* (Dallas: Word, 1985), 155.

16. David Otis Fuller, *Spurgeon's Sermon Notes* (Grand Rapids: Zondervan, n.d.), 287.

17. Ibid.

18. Ravi Zacharias, *Deliver Us from Evil* (Dallas: Word, 1996), 151–53.

Chapter Two—Whose Kingdom Are You Building?

1. Ravi Zacharias, *Deliver Us from Evil* (Dallas: Word, 1996), 197–98.

2. Deion Sanders, *Power, Money, and Sex* (Nashville: Word, 1998), cover.

3. Ibid., 186.

4. Adapted from Bob Moorehead, *How to Counsel Yourself and Others from the Bible* (Portland, Ore: Multnomah, 1994), 14.

5. Walter A. Elwell, *The Concise Evangelical Dictionary of Theology* (Grand Rapids: Baker, 1991), 480–81.

6. George Sweeting, *Great Quotes and Illustrations* (Dallas: Word, 1985), 130.

7. Elwell, *Dictionary,* 481.

8. J. Oswald Sanders, *Spiritual Leadership* (Chicago: Moody Press, 1967), 25–26.

9. Edythe Draper, *Draper's Book of Quotations for the Christian World* (Wheaton, Ill.: Tyndale, 1992), 585.

10. Philip Yancey, *The Jesus I Never Knew* (Grand Rapids: Zondervan, 1995), 109.

11. William Barclay, *The Gospel of Mark* (Philadelphia: Westminster, 1975), 255.

12. Ibid.

13. Draper, *Quotations,* 597.

14. Ibid., 593.

15. Ibid.

16. James Patterson and Peter Kim, *The Day America Told the Truth* (New York: Plume, 1992), 27–28.

17. Ibid., 598.

18. Sweeting, *Great Quotes,* 230.

19. Malcolm Muggeridge, *The End of Christendom* (Grand Rapids: Eerdmans, 1980), 52–53: quoted in Zacharias, *Deliver Us from Evil,* 84.

20. Draper, *Quotations,* 560.

Chapter Three—Who Sets Your Agenda?

1. Martin E. Marty, *Evangelicals and the Cultural Mainstream*, Public Religion Project, 919 N. Michigan Ave., Ste. 540, Chicago, IL 60611, 12 August 1998. The research on evangelicalism in America was done by Mark A. Shibley of Southern Oregon University in the Annals of the American Academy of Political and Social Sciences (July 1998).

2. We are not competing with other nations to see who is evangelizing most; however, America has been used in a unique way to promote the gospel throughout the world. Because of compromise in the standards of holiness and lethargy in communicating the gospel to every nation and people, the denominations of this country could become much less of an influence on world evangelization. History records examples of this happening to other denominations and nations.

3. Herbert F. Stevenson, *The Ministry of Keswick: The Risen Lord in His Personal Glory* (Grand Rapids: Zondervan, 1964), 224.

4. George Sweeting, *Great Quotes and Illustrations* (Waco, Tex.: Word, 1985), 128.

5. Abridged from James Bilton, "God Doesn't Play Games," *Pentecostal Evangel*, 6 July 1997, 4–5. Used by permission.

6. Sweeting, *Great Quotes*, 128.

7. Abridged from Thomas E. Trask and Wayde I. Goodall, *Back to the Word* (Springfield, Mo.: Gospel Publishing House, 1996), 46–47.

8. Ibid., 160.

9. Michael P. Green, ed., *Illustrations for Biblical Preaching* (Grand Rapids: Baker, 1982), 35.

10. Ted W. Engstrom and Norman B. Rohrer, *Making the Right Choices* (Nashville: Thomas Nelson, 1993), 143–44. Used by permission.

11. George Barna, "Trends of Significance," *Barna Report*, January/February 1998, 5.

Chapter Four—The Beginning of the End

1. Neither Wayde nor I saw the movie because of the rating and the unnecessary nude scene.

2. Bob McAllister, "From My Perspective," *Family News in Focus*: quoted in *The Pastor's Weekly Briefing* 6, no. 6 (6 February 1998), 2.

3. Cited in *Current Thoughts and Trends*, July 1977, 23. In contrast, Barna found that adult attendance at Sunday school jumped from 17 percent in 1996 to 23 percent last year. (*Emerging Trends*, March 1997, 1; *The Pastor's Weekly Briefing*, 11 April 1997, 2).

4. H. B. London, "Market Share," *The Pastor's Weekly Briefing* 6, no. 24 (12 June 1998), 1.

5. Anonymous, "Why We're Here," *Pentecostal Evangel*, 20 September 1998, 5.

6. David Wilkerson, "The Forgotten, Lost Multitudes!" *Times Square Church Pulpit Series*, 30 June 1997, 1. Used by permission.

7. Ibid.

8. H. B. London, "In God We Trust," *The Pastor's Weekly Briefing* 6, no. 18 (1 May 1998), 1.

9. George Otis Jr., as quoted by Howard Fultz at the National Symposium on Postdenominational Church, 22 May 1996: quoted in *Ministry Advantage* 6, no. 4 (July/August 1996), 8.

10. Thomas E. Trask and Wayde I. Goodall, *The Blessing: Experiencing the Power of the Holy Spirit Today* (Grand Rapids: Zondervan, 1998), 176–78.

11. Joel Kilpatrick, interview with Jaci Velasquez, *Pentecostal Evangel*, 13 September 1998, 6.

12. H. B. London, "With or Without," *The Pastor's Weekly Briefing* 6, no. 35 (28 August 1998), 1.

13. *Current Thoughts and Trends*, February 1997, 1.

14. Source unknown: quoted in "Our Global Village," *Ministry Advantage* 6, no. 4 (July/August 1996), 8.

Chapter Five—The Look of Love

1. Abridged from Dan Van Veen, "Only Jesus," *American Horizon*, September/October 1998, 8–9. Used by permission.

2. George Sweeting, *Special Sermons* (Chicago: Moody Press, 1985), 698.

3. Abridged from Doug Brendel, *Aggie* (Springfield, Mo.: Gospel Publishing House, 1986).

4. Edythe Draper, *Draper's Book of Quotations for the Christian World* (Wheaton, Ill.: Tyndale, 1992), 397.

5. Ibid., 392.

6. Ibid., 397.

7. Ibid.

8. Charles Arn, "The Love Quotient: Measuring Quality Growth," *Ministry Advantage* 7, no. 2 (March/April 1997), 10, citing the book *Who Cares About Love?* by Win Arn, Carroll Nyquist, and Charles Arn (Pasadena, Calif.: Church Growth Press, 1988).

9. Ibid.

10. Abridged from Arn, "The Love Quotient," 10–11.

11. Quoted in Richard John Neuhaus, *Freedom for Ministry* (Grand Rapids: Eerdmans, 1992), 119.

12. Warren W. Wiersbe, *Being a Child of God* (Nashville: Thomas Nelson, 1996), 100.

Chapter Six—Paradise Lost

1. "Dying Wonder," *Pentecostal Evangel,* 1 March 1998, 5.

2. C. S. Lewis, *The Screwtape Letters* (New York: Touchstone, 1982), 127–28.

3. Walt Mueller, "Marilyn Manson's Revenge," *New Man,* September/October 1998, 34. Reprinted with permission of *New Man*, September/October 1988, Strang Communications Co., USA.

4. Ibid.

5. Ibid., 32–33. We have abridged Mueller's quote. Used by permission.

6. Billy Graham, *Facing Death and the Life After* (Dallas: Word, 1987), 217.

7. Ibid., 219.

8. Ibid., 220.

9. H. L. Mencken, *A New Dictionary of Quotations* (New York: Alfred A. Knopf, 1966), 68.

10. George Barna, *Evangelism That Works* (Ventura, Calif.: Regal, 1995), 27–28. Used by permission.

11. Philip Yancey, "Heaven Can't Wait," *Christianity Today,* 7 September 1984: quoted in Billy Graham, *Facing Death and the Life After* (Waco, Tex.: Word, 1987), 221.

12. Ibid.

13. This experience happened to Wayde I. Goodall. The names and some details have been changed to protect the confidentiality of the families involved.

Chapter Seven—God's Strategic Plan

1. Billy Graham, "The King Is Coming," in *Let the Earth Hear His Voice*, Official Reference Volume for the International Congress on World Evangelization, Lausanne, Switzerland, ed. J. D. Douglas (Minneapolis: World Wide Publications, 1975), 1466.

2. "Global Revival," *Ministry Advantage* 7, no. 2 (March/April 1997), 30 (Statistics were drawn from the following sources: Frank Damazio, *Seasons of Intercession* [Portland Ore.: BT Publishing, 1996], 50–52; *Mission Frontier* [November/December 1996]; *Charisma* [January 1996], 31–34; and *Charisma* [January 1997], 30–34.)

3. Revival is typically identified when Christians sense they need to repent of any ungodly habits or lifestyles and have heightened desire to evangelize the lost. It is also identified when a large ingathering of non-Christians have become Christians. A third characteristic of revival is the hunger for the Word of God among believers. Worldwide we see evidence of revival. There are pockets of revival in the United States; however, the kind of church growth that is happening in countries like Korea, Argentina, Brazil, Russia, and China are not evident at this time in America. We must pray for America that revival would impact all of the church of this land.

4. Michael Slaughter, "Essential Principles for Church Renewal," *Ministry Advantage* 7, no. 2 (March/April 1997), 4.

5. *New York Times Book Review* reported in its issue of December 30, 1979, that *The Late Great Planet Earth* was the biggest-selling nonfiction book during the decade of the seventies.

6. Robert E. Coleman, *The Coming World Revival* (Wheaton, Ill.: Crossway, 1995), 156.

7. Billy Graham, *Storm Warning* (Dallas: Word, 1992), 36–37.

8. Quoted in Graham, *Storm Warning*, 195.

9. Ibid.

10. Graham, *Storm Warning*, 196–97.

11. Ibid., 200.

12. Ibid., 197–98.

13. Thomas E. Trask and Wayde I. Goodall, *The Battle: Defeating the Enemies of Your Soul* (Grand Rapids: Zondervan, 1997), 158–60.

14. Graham, *Storm Warning*, 36–37.

15. Coleman, *Coming World Revival*, 155.

16. *The Life Millennium: The 100 Most Important Events and People of the Past 1,000 Years* (New York: Life Books, Time Inc., 1998), 58.

17. Ibid., 42.

18. Ibid., 189.

19. Ibid., 188.

20. John Phillips, *Exploring the Future* (Neptune, N.J.: Loizeaux, 1992), 376.

21. Coleman, *Coming World Revival*, 156–57.

Chapter Eight—Show and Tell

1. This experience happened to Wayde I. Goodall while serving as pastor of Vienna Christian Center, Vienna, Austria.

2. Paul Little with Dale and Sandy Larsen, *How to Give Away Your Faith* (Downers Grove, Ill.: InterVarsity Press, 1996), 19.

3. Donald Stamps, *The Full Life Study Bible* (Grand Rapids: Zondervan, 1992), 1618.

4. George Barna, "Evangelism and Accountability," *Barna Report* 1, no. 6, 4.

5. George Barna, *Evangelism That Works* (Ventura, Calif.: Regal, 1995), 71–73. Used by permission.

6. H. B. London, "Waiting for the Holy Spirit," *Pastor to Pastor*, vol. 37, September/October 1998, 3.

7. C. P. Wagner, "Characteristics of Pentecostal Church Growth," in L. Grant McClung, ed., *Azusa Street and Beyond* (North Brunswick, N.J.: Bridge-Logos, 1986), 129: quoted in Wonsuk Ma and Robert Menzies, *Pentecostalism in Context* (Sheffield, England: Sheffield Academic Press, 1997), 190.

8. Ibid.

9. J. I. Packer, *Keep in Step with the Spirit* (Grand Rapids: Revell, 1984), 28: quoted in Wonsuk and Menzies, *Pentecostalism in Context*, 190.

10. Thomas E. Trask and Wayde I. Goodall, *The Blessing: Experiencing the Power of the Holy Spirit Today* (Grand Rapids: Zondervan, 1998), 83–85.

11. Rick Warren, *The Purpose Driven Church* (Grand Rapids: Zondervan, 1995), 189.

12. George Barna, "The Top 100: Part 1," *Barna Report*, May/June 1997, 4.

13. Compiled from information provided in Barna, "The Top 100: Part 1."

14. C. Peter Wagner, "Does Your Church Have Koinonitis?" *Ministries Today* 15, no. 3 (May/June 1997), 33–35.

15. Little, *How to Give Away Your Faith*, 41.

16. Ibid., 2.

17. *Family News from Dr. James Dobson*, Focus on the Family (August 1998), 2.

18. Abridged from Don Spradling, "Sharing Jesus on the Links," *Pentecostal Evangel*, 11 October 1998, 6.

Chapter Nine—Improving the Odds

1. Abridged from Leith Anderson, *A Church for the 21st Century* (Minneapolis: Bethany House, 1992), 216.

2. D. James Kennedy, *Evangelism Explosion*, 4th ed. (Wheaton, Ill.: Tyndale, 1996), 103.

3. William Barclay, *The Gospel of John* (Philadelphia: Westminster, 1975), 230.

4. Bill Bright, *Five Steps to Making Disciples* (Orlando: New Life Publications, 1997), 6.

5. Barclay, *John,* 229 (abridged).

6. Quoted in *Current Thoughts and Trends*, October 1998, 4.

7. Bright, *Five Steps,* 6. Italics added.

8. Kennedy, *Evangelism Explosion,* 103.

9. Ibid., 6.

10. Ibid., 7.

11. I am grateful for Rick Warren's willingness to permit the denomination I serve to develop a program for our churches that utilizes the principles he teaches in his book. We have retooled it and called it "We Build People."

12. Rick Warren, *The Purpose-Driven® Church* (Grand Rapids: Zondervan, 1995), 103.

13. George Sweeting, *Great Quotes and Illustrations* (Dallas: Word, 1985), 269.

14. Warren, *Purpose Driven Church,* 104.

15. C. Peter Wagner, "Knowing the Vital Signs," *Ministry Advantage* 7, no. 4, 11.

16. Edythe Draper, *Draper's Book of Quotations for the Christian World* (Wheaton, Ill.: Tyndale, 1992), 155.

17. Warren, *Purpose Driven Church,* 104.

18. Ibid., 105.

19. Ibid., 103–7.

20. Draper, *Quotations,* 156.

21. Quoted in David Wilkerson, *Times Square Church Pulpit Series,* 5 October 1998.

22. Ibid.

23. For further reading on the topic of speaking in other tongues, please see our book, *The Blessing: Experiencing the Power of the Holy Spirit Today* (Grand Rapids: Zondervan, 1998), chap. 3.

24. For further reading, see our book *The Battle: Defeating the Enemies of Your Soul* (Grand Rapids: Zondervan, 1997).

25. Sweeting, *Great Quotes,* 246.

26. Donald Grey Barnhouse, *Let Me Illustrate* (Grand Rapids: Revell, 1967), 317.

27. Draper, *Quotations,* 156.

28. Adapted from *Current Thoughts and Trends*, February 1997, 18: summarized from Davis Duggins, "Future of Missions: Good News and Bad," *Moody*, November/December 1996, 14–18.

Chapter Ten—The Devil's Last Day Strategy

1. Billy Graham, *Storm Warning* (Dallas: Word, 1992), 143.

2. Author Monte Leach in his commentary *Tara Center–Northern California*. Note: We do not recommend that young Christians contact this New Age religious center.

3. "Inflation: Who Is Hurt Worst?" *Time*, 15 January 1979: quoted in Michael P. Green, *Illustrations for Biblical Preaching* (Grand Rapids: Baker, 1989), 21.

4. George Sweeting, *Great Quotes and Illustrations* (Dallas: Word, 1985), 17–18.

5. List of names found in Michael W. Holmes, *The NIV Application Commentary* (Grand Rapids: Zondervan, 1998), 241.

6. C. S. Lewis, *The Screwtape Letters* (New York: Touchstone, 1982).

7. See our book *The Battle: Defeating the Enemies of Your Soul* (Grand Rapids: Zondervan, 1997).

8. William R. Mattox Jr., "Hell Deserves as Much Respect as Heaven," *USA Today*, 29 October 1998, 15A.

9. Author unknown.

10. James Dobson, *Family News from Dr. James Dobson*, August 1998, 2.

11. Cathy Hainer, "The New Face of Witches," *USA Today*, 29 October 1998, 8D.

12. Ibid.

13. *Prayer for the Persecuted Church*, 2025 Arlington Heights Rd., Ste. 113, Arlington Heights, IL 60005.

14. Edythe Draper, *Draper's Book of Quotations for the Christian World* (Wheaton, IL: Tyndale, 1992), 147.

15. Steve Haus, *Shatter the Silence*, brochure, P.O. Box WEF, Wheaton, IL 60189.

16. Information on persecuted Christians taken from the 1998 International Day of Prayer for the Persecuted Church. For more information, please contact *Shatter the Silence*, Steve Haus, P.O. Box WEF, Wheaton, IL 60189.

17. Haus, *Shatter the Silence*.

18. Alex Buchan et al., "The Holy Spirit Is Moving Powerfully Around the Globe," *Charisma*, January 1998: quoted in *Current*

Thoughts and Trends, April 1998, 29.

19. Ben Taylor, "CBS Sends Mixed Message on Morality," *Citizen* 12, no. 5 (May 1998), 5.

20. H. B. London, "The Culture War," *The Pastor's Weekly Briefing*, 30 October 1998, 2.

21. Abridged from David Wilkerson's *Times Square Pulpit Series*, 30 March 1998, 3.

22. James Dobson, "Disintegration of Moral Leadership," *Wireless Age*, June/July/August 1998, 24.

23. George Barna, "The Results Are In," *Barna Report*, Premiere Issue, 6.

24. Ibid.

25. Quoted in David Reagan, "The Most Dangerous Doctrine in Christianity Today," *Lamplighter* 18, no. 7 (July 1997), 1.

26. Draper, *Quotations*, 149.

Chapter Eleven—The Millennial Mandate

1. News release, "Billy Graham Announces 'Amsterdam 2000,'" Billy Graham Evangelistic Association, Minneapolis, 15 September 1998.

2. Luis Palau, "Which Part of the Great Commission Don't You Understand?" *Christianity Today*, 16 November 1998, 76.

3. George Otis, "Invasion from the Dark Side," *Charisma* 22, no. 8 (March 1997), 50–58: quoted in *Current Thoughts and Trends*, June 1997, 27.

4. David Barrett, "A Century of Growth," *Christianity Today*, 16 November 1998, 50–51.

5. Ibid., 50.

6. Mark Hutchinson, "It's a Small Church After All," *Christianity Today*, 16 November 1998, 46–47.

7. Charles Dunahoo, "The Church's Challenge—Reaching the Millennials," *Equip for Ministry* 4, no. 4 (July/August 1998), 7–10: quoted in *Current Thoughts and Trends*, November 1998, 20.

8. Ibid.

9. The word *nation* comes from the Greek word *ethne* (from which we derive the word *ethnic*). *Ethne* means "an ethnic or cultural group of people." Missiologists use the term *people group*.

10. Billy Graham, "Standing firm, Moving Forward," *Christianity Today* 40, no. 10 (September 16, 1996), 14–15: quoted in *Current Thoughts and Trends*, December 1996, 22.

11. Thomas E. Trask and Wayde I. Goodall, *The Battle: Defeating the Enemy of Your Soul* (Grand Rapids: Zondervan, 1997), 149–50.

12. HealthCare Ministries are part of The Division of Foreign Missions, Assemblies of God, Springfield, Missouri.

13. Luis Palau, "Which Part of the Great Commission Don't You Understand?" *Christianity Today*, 16 November 1998, 76.

14. Ted Haggard is pastor of New Life Church in Colorado Springs. He told the story of David Hogan in a presentation at the National Symposium on the Postdenominational Church, 22 May 1996. Found in *Ministry Advantage* 6, no. 4 (July/August 1996), 8.

15. Alex Buchan, Camilla Luckey, Pat Chen, Mauricio Tupinamba, Tomas Dixon, Julia Duin, Francisco Palafox, Tessie DeVore, "Miracles Still Happen," *Charisma* 23, no. 6 (January 1998), 38–94: quoted in *Current Thoughts and Trends*, April 1998, 29.

16. Ibid.

17. Ibid.

18. George Otis Jr., "Exponential Harvest," *Ministry Advantage*, July/August 1996, 8.

19. David Bryant, "Prisoners of Hope," *New Man* 13, no. 6 (September 1996), 30–35: quoted in *Current Thoughts and Trends*, October 1996, 5.

20. For more information about The Jesus Film Project contact: Campus Crusade for Christ, P.O. Box 72007, San Clemente, CA 92674.

21. *Current Thoughts and Trends*, July 1996, 29.

22. D. James Kennedy, *Evangelism Explosion*, 4th ed. (Wheaton, Ill.: Tyndale, 1996), xi–xii.

23. Mission America, 901 East 78th Street, Minneapolis, MN 55420.

24. H. B. London, *The Pastor's Weekly Briefing*, 13 February 1998, 1.

25. Joel Kilpatrick, "Food Ministry Seeks Bigger, Broader Impact," *Christianity Today*, 16 November 1998, 26.

26. *National and International Religion Report*, 29 April 1996, 6: quoted in *Current Thoughts and Trends*, July 1996, 29.

27. Neil Anderson, "Signs of a Worldwide Great Awakening," *Ministry Advantage* 7, no. 2 (March/April 1997).

28. Palau, "Which Part of the Great Commission Don't You Understand?" 74.

29. Ibid.

Scripture Index